1985

The Future of the Printed Word

The Future of the Printed Word

The Impact and the Implications of the
New Communications Technology

edited by Philip Hills

Greenwood Press
Westport, Connecticut

Library of Congress Cataloging in Publication Data
Main entry under title:

The future of the printed word.

1. Publishers and publishing—Automation—
Addresses, essays, lectures. 2. Printing—Addresses,
essays, lectures. 3. Information networks—Addresses,
essays, lectures. 4. Information storage and
retrieval systems—Addresses, essays, lectures.
5. Micrographics—Addresses, essays, lectures.
6. Communication—Addresses, essays, lectures.
I. Hills, Philip James.
Z278.F87   070.5'028'54   80-1716
ISBN 0-313-22693-8 (lib. bdg.)

Copyright © 1980 by P. J. Hills

First published 1980

Published in the United States and Canada by
Greenwood Press
A division of Congressional Information Service, Inc.
Westport, Connecticut

English language edition, except the United States and Canada,
published by Frances Pinter (Publishers) Limited

Library of Congress Catalog Card Number: 80-1716

ISBN: 0-313-22693-8

Printed in Great Britain

CONTENTS

PREFACE

This is a book of readings by a group of specialists in the fields of publishing, librarianship, information science, computing and education. Each author was invited to contribute a paper in his or her particular area of expertise giving perceptions of the future of the printed word.

Although this book is concerned to a great extent with print on paper, and the way in which it may be displaced by or act as a supplement to the new communications technology, or find its own particular niche in our society, it is also concerned with any composition of words in a readable form, whether as a videodisplay, as a printout from a computer or from microfiche or film.

Whatever the new methods bring, however, one thing is certain — people will still be required to read. It therefore seems appropriate that the last word in this set of readings is given by R.J. Heathorn in an article which appeared in *Punch* on 9 May 1962 entitled "Learn with BOOK" (reproduced here with permission) and dealing with that new device 'Built-in Orderly Organized Knowledge'.

The Future of the Printed Word is intended to be a first statement in an area of ever-growing importance in the 1980s.

A book of readings of this kind can result from the proceedings of a conference, but often the valuable part of a conference is the discussion it provokes outside the formal sessions. Books are traditionally used as a one-way flow of information but this need not be so. It should be possible for one book to act in the same way as the formal session of a conference, to be followed closely by a second publication which might report discussion of the topics from the first and give further articles to update these topics. Books can be produced and distributed rapidly today, and since at present the printed book can reach a large audience, far larger than any of the new technologies, perhaps this is a good and legitimate use of the printed word.

When you read this book, react to the articles as you might to papers in a conference, then contact me with any comments, observations or additional material which you feel should be added to balance the picture or extend the range of information presented.

If your response is sufficient and reasonably rapid, then a second volume can result, a volume which will not only extend and amplify this area of concern but will also illustrate yet one further and possible future use of the printed word.

P.J. Hills
Leicester
April 1980

1. FUTURE METHODS AND TECHNIQUES

JOHN M. STRAWHORN
Vitro Laboratories Division,
Automation Industries, Inc., USA

Introduction

Forecasting is a difficult, error-prone business. Under the best of conditions, even short-range forecasts are likely to contain significant errors, and the more deeply one tries to look into the future, the greater the likelihood that the forecast will be wrong. All the commonly used approaches to forecasting (trend analysis, Delphi technique, extrapolation and projection, and so on) are subject to this limitation, despite the use of many techniques to reduce the degree of error (Argenti, 1971). The reasons for this are, at least in broad outline, obvious. Our only bases for forecasting derive from our knowledge of the past and present, which is imperfect and incomplete. Also, some events and conditions will inevitably arise that are discontinuous with the past, or at least could not have been foreseen. All of these factors can confound the forecaster.

There are arguments, though, for the attempt to forecast. First, in spite of its frailty, forecasting is a necessary activity (Steiner, 1969). In an environment that is changing as rapidly as ours, we simply must try to position ourselves for the future, and this entails forecasting. If we approach it properly, we can minimize its grossest weaknesses. Whatever its imperfections, we shall find forecasting preferable to the alternative (Bell, 1973).

Second, forecasting is, or should be, an iterative process. A forecast that is made, then left alone, will surely prove increasingly inaccurate as time passes. If, however, we review and revise our forecasts at fairly frequent intervals, we can fine-

13

tune them, allowing, in each new cycle, for those elements that were previously unforeseen.

Third, if we are trying to forecast technology or technology-dependent developments, we do have some tools at our disposal. Despite current appearances, technological innovations do not develop and diffuse overnight. Since it is likely to take anything from five to twenty years or more for an innovation to become widely accepted, a good knowledge of technology's 'leading edge', coupled with an understanding of the environment and the factors that are likely to be conducive to success, will at least provide a basis for informed speculation about the future. We know that the speculation will err in many of its particulars, but if approached properly it should be accurate enough to be useful.

In this article I shall try to sidestep some of the pitfalls of forecasting by maintaining the discussion on a fairly general level. I shall not attempt to predict specific devices, methods or techniques, but will endeavour to review general classes of methods and techniques currently under development or in process of diffusion. I shall also offer some thoughts as to their impact and direction as they undergo further refinement and diffusion. My main purpose will be to look for the meaning in the new methods and techniques.

The impact of the information explosion

The enormous growth in the amount of recorded information, which — especially in science and technology — is often referred to as 'the information explosion', is usually considered a problem primarily for libraries and for information storage and retrieval systems. Beyond this, it is recognized as a source of the individual scholar's or professional's difficulty in 'keeping up' with developments of interest. It is not usually seen as a problem for authors or publishers, nor one that overarches our entire communications system. I believe, however, that it is actually a higher-order problem, with important implications for every stakeholder in the system of information transfer, that it has already played an important role in the development of the new methods and techniques now in use (especially the 'new technology'), and that it will play an increasingly important role in the development of new methods and techniques as time passes. It would behove authors and primary publishers, just as much as librarians and bibliographic processors, to understand the information explosion and its consequences.

The information explosion is a simple function of size and growth. As Price pointed out, the population of scientists (and the same probably applies to other learned professions as well, since it applies to population generally) has been growing exponentially throughout most of our history. Hence his well-known statement that 'eighty to ninety percent of all the scientists that have ever lived are alive now' (Price, 1963). One feature of exponential growth is that, through starting from small absolute values, it goes unnoticed for a long time. At a certain point, when the values begin to become very large, the exponentially growing thing appears to observers almost to explode, though its rate of growth is in fact no greater than it was originally (Price, 1961).

Applying this model to the printed word, we can probably say that printed information has been growing at an exponential rate, doubling perhaps every fifteen years, at least since the days of Gutenberg, but it was not until sometime in the mid-twentieth century that the growth became large enough to be noticed. The passing of this 'threshold of observability' was, I submit, a matter of profound importance. Why should this be?

The human brain's storage capacity has often been remarked on, usually in awesome terms (e.g. by Asimov, 1972). Whatever it may be, though, the brain's storage capacity is in any case finite, and barring some major breakthroughs in brain research we really have little reason to suppose that scientists, engineers, scholars and other 'knowledge workers' could stuff vastly larger quantities of information into their heads than they now do. We must remember, too, that the brain is limited at input (by the process of reading or other method of ingestion of information), and in its functioning as a retrieval, as well as a storage, system.

We know, therefore, that the brain is limited in several ways in its ability to acquire, store, process, and output information.

As we shall see, the information explosion confronts us with these limitations. In doing so, it forces us to develop a new way of dealing with information, an altered relationship between the user and the information he uses.

Until quite recently, the dominant model in information use was one of pre-ingestion and pre-digestion. In the course of their education and training, people learned the bulk of what they would need to know in their subsequent professional activity. The process might be rather extended, but it was both leisurely and purposeful; there was little question as to what information would be required in the course of one's career. After the basic educational or training experience, one would certainly acquire increased skill as well as some additional knowledge, but this was generally secondary to the application of what had already been learned.

This pattern is no longer possible; the knowledge base is simply too large. One of the first effects of the now greatly expanded quantity of information was the development of specialization. The familiar saw, that a specialist is someone who learns more and more about less and less until he knows everything about nothing, carries its hint of derogation because it misses the fundamental point. There is simply so much to know about so many things that *nobody* can encompass everything known about a major field (such as medicine or physics) (Bell, 1973). Faced with this problem, the first response is usually to segment the field, learn it in summary or outline form, and concentrate on a subfield in detail.

In many cases, however, we have passed the point at which our traditional model of information use can be applied even within the narrowed confines that specialization provides. We might term this condition a second-order result of the information explosion. Now, since we cannot completely cover our fields or subfields, we must initially learn that which is basic and of overriding importance about our general fields, learn still more about our subfield specialities, and then learn how to find everything else we may need to know. We cannot complete our substantive knowledge; we must acknowledge its incompleteness and supplement it with the ability to extend it as particular conditions require.

Two things, therefore, have changed. First, there is the rather obvious requirement for improved access to information. This implies the processing of information in ways which will permit its subsequent location and retrieval, the development of systems to support the user in accessing and obtaining the information, and the development of new skills on the user's part. Second, though, and of equal importance, is the fact that we are now talking about using information *in a new way*.

The information is now consumed, not for use at some time in the future, but on the spot, because of an immediate requirement. These conditions of use typically carry much greater urgency and specificity than our classical model can handle. Because of this fundamental change in the conditions of use, the attributes of the information and the way in which it is delivered will almost certainly need to differ from those that were acceptable under the traditional system. I will return to this point later, when we will see that it has bearing on both the technologies and the concepts that we use in printed communication.

Agents and functions in information transfer

The model described in Figure 1 (adapted from Strawhorn et al., 1977) provides a general description of the communications system that concerns us. It was developed with scientific and technical communication specifically in mind, but it can accommodate other kinds of scholarly and professional information transfer. The model shows the flow of information from one function to another, with some of the principal agents responsible for those functions indicated. Each function presents certain intellectual, technical and practical problems. What is surprising and impressive is the extent to which new methods and techniques have been developed to deal with the entire array of these functions. Space does not permit us an extended discussion of these individual methods and techniques, nor in fact is it the main purpose of this article, since we are more interested in the area and nature of impact. Consider, however, the following methods and techniques, and the functions to which they can be applied:

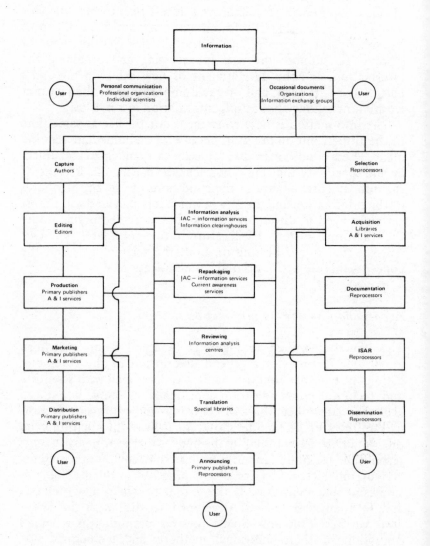

Figure 1. Flow model of information transfer.

Methods and techniques	*Areas of impact*
1. Electronic document creation and editing (includes word processing and computerized text editing)	Capture, editing and production
2. Photocomposition	Production, repackaging
3. New imaging and reprographic techniques (such as electronic printing)	Production, repackaging, distribution, dissemination of reprocessed information
4. Electronic communications (including electronic mail)	Transfer points among all agents in the system
5. New recording, storage and retrieval systems (holographic storage, bubble memories and so on)	Multiple functions, including all those that require storage and retrieval of information; some may also be used as media for distribution
6. New packaging and delivery concepts (such as synopsis publishing, information mapping, cumulative monographs, electronic journals)	Pervasive
7. Computers, including mainframes, minicomputers and microprocessors	Pervasive

This very brief glance at new developments and their areas of application begins to show why we have the feeling of being in the midst of a revolution. New technology — much of it electronic or related to electronics — is being developed for every segment of our system of communication through the printed word. Although the development and diffusion of new concepts for the packaging and delivery of information are lagging behind the technology, it is certain that such sweeping technological changes will encourage new concepts and new modes of communication.

Some of the items mentioned above (such as holographic storage systems) are still under development, or for some other reason have yet to be brought to market. Some may never get that far, or may not find widespread acceptance. It is interesting — and sometimes important — to speculate on which possibilities will succeed. Rogers and Shoemaker (1971) postulate five 'perceived attributes' that determine an innovation's prospects for acceptance:

1. Relative advantage (the degree to which the innovation is perceived as offering an improvement over the idea it supersedes);
2. Compatibility with the adopter's past experience and current value system:
3. Complexity;
4. 'Trialability' (the degree to which the innovation lends itself to trial on a limited scale);
5. Observability (the clarity with which the results of adoption can be seen).

I would suggest that two attributes should be added to this list: (1) the cost of implementation and (2) what I would call a 'risk/commitment' factor, which has to do with the extent to which potential adopters see themselves as being 'locked in' to the innovation following its implementation. (It is easier to decide to do something when we know that we can change our minds if it does not work out).

These several attributes could be quantified for most potential innovations, at least in a rough, subjective way. They should be helpful in predicting a particular innovation's prospects for success, but I believe they may also leave some important dimensions unaddressed. For example, many questions surround the potential *application* of an innovation. One such question concerns the application's importance, and this may draw widely divergent responses from different potential adopters, or even from the same people at different times. In addition, an extremely difficult case to deal with is the innovation whose function is largely discontinuous with the past: that is, an innovation that does not clearly replace some previous idea or thing, but, in a sense, brings its own application with it (xerography is to some extent an example of this). Nonetheless, the attributes identified above, and perhaps a few others, should have considerable value in predicting the degree of acceptance that an innovation will find among a particular group of users.

The impact of new methods and techniques

As I have suggested, the new methods and techniques that have been developed and diffused to date have been more technological than conceptual. Even so, the sum of the new technologies — which we may well call, without fear of exaggeration, the 'electronic revolution' — has not fully manifested itself. The impact *intended* by its adopters has been primarily to facilitate the functions we have already described. In other words, these electronic tools — word processing, photocomposition, computer networks and the like — have in most cases been adopted with a view to "fine-tuning" the current system of communication. The adopters have generally sought simply to facilitate the discharge of their responsibilities within the system with which we are all familiar.

At a deeper level, however — and I am by no means the first to remark on this — the new technologies have begun to work profound changes. The first of these has been to alter the nature of the basic product. In all traditional technologies, the printed word was the one and only product. One book might be used to produce another, but the process had to be repeated.

When computers began to be used to drive photocomposers, this changed. The digital file which was used to create the image of the printed word could be used to recreate that process; it could also be manipulated and used for other purposes. The fundamental product, in fact, was now a database. It was no longer the printed word, but a precise, manipulable, compact record which could be used with considerable flexibility for various applications.

This change is an important link in the chain of events that has already led to substantial alterations in the way the words we read are created, and that will undoubtedly lead us into realms yet undiscovered. We should not be misled by the relatively traditional appearance of most of the printed products with which we deal. The new technology can create familiar-looking products, but it also makes possible ways of presenting and disseminating information that were previously unthinkable. We already have enormous user-searchable bibliographic and numeric databases stored on interactive computer systems, as well as electronic message systems. In those cases, users can see the difference between new and traditional forms. In other cases, the difference is not so obvious. Structured textiles, such as dictionaries, can be revised, subdivided, and reused with a degree of flexibility never before known. By creating user interest profiles, we can create systems for the selective dissemination of individual articles; only the computer makes this practical.

The first major impact of the new technology, then, is the development, or the groundwork for the development, of an electronic literature. The term *literature* must be used here quite loosely, since the characteristics and capabilities of computer processing make possible 'literatures' quite unlike those we are used to, even while they allow the production of specific packages of information that are quite conventional in appearance.

A second major trend is also under way. The electronic revolution is concerned not only with the creation, storage, retrieval and use of databases. It is also concerned with their transmission from one point or party to another. Given the necessary electronic linkages, which may be nothing more than conventional telephone lines, text or data files which can be created on a word processor or computer in one location can be quickly and accurately transmitted electronically to a compatible device in another location. The term *compatible* is by no means trivial, and communication of this type is still in its infancy. It has already progressed, though, to a point at which we can see its significance, and it portends important developments for the future. During the next few years the interconnection of electronic systems (word processors, computers and so on) will be one of the major 'growth areas' of the electronic revolution.

A third major trend is an alteration in the roles of various agents in the system and a modification of the relationships that exist among them. This comes from the *combination* of the first two, coupled with the general trends observable in electronics: increased processing power and flexibility, progressive miniaturization of equipment, a tendency toward integration or convergence of different systems, and diminishing costs. Authors, for example, can now create machine-readable records that will drive photocomposers to produce typeset copy. In days gone by, typesetting was a function that fell squarely and exclusively within the domain of the publisher. The author now has a distinctly larger measure of responsibility for the final appearance of his work. Indeed, it is increasingly likely that the author may have access to a typesetting device. Because of the role computers now play in composition, it is no longer necessary to have complicated, special skills to operate these devices. The author may be able to produce the kind of professional-looking copy for which he previously needed the publisher. (This is an exaggeration, but a relatively modest one). If the author has access to a laser printer or other appropriate reprographic device, he may be able to provide the end user with finished copy. Author and user may be able to communicate with each other through electronic channels, bypassing many of the linkages in the traditional system.

These changes tend to encourage a do-it-yourself approach to communication, with the author (and the friendly computer) acting as publisher. They call into question the need for publishers as intermediaries. If, however, we reflect seriously on the publisher's contributions, we find that most of them are concerned with the establishment and preservation of quality in the system of formal communication. These contributions can probably not be replaced by authors and users acting on their own behalf. Nonetheless, the new technology will encourage an expanded system of informal and semiformal communication that will mimic some of the external characteristics of what we know as formal publishing. It will also force a thorough re-examination of the roles of publishers and other intermediaries.

There is a final area of major impact. I mentioned earlier that the information explosion has presented us with the necessity of finding a new way of dealing with professional information. The technologies we have been considering provide us with the tools we need for this: they allow us to store, manipulate and retrieve information with a high degree of flexibility. They are the instruments which are making it possible to effect a transition from a society based on pre-learning to one that depends on the instant acquisition of information from databases as it is needed. One sign of this transition is the enormous growth in the scope and use of large-scale bibliographic online search services, which in several cases now include provision for the ordering of documents discovered through the user's search of relevant databases. This kind of development can only be a beginning, however. It still rests for the most part on traditional ways of packaging and presenting information, which were not developed to satisfy the requirements of the information age.

The future of the printed word

In this book, the expression *printed word* is construed very broadly, to include words in any kind of display: paper, microforms, CRTs, plasma panels and so on. When we construe the term in this sweeping way, it is obvious that the printed word has a long future. Herein though lies a point that the enthusiast of electronic communication and new media all too often overlooks: no matter how the information is transmitted and displayed, no matter what kinds of exotic technology we employ, people will *still be reading*. If we really wish to improve *communication*, then, we must attend to much more than the tools whereby words are recorded, moved from one place to another, and presented to a consumer of information. We need to learn how best to get information out of one person's head and into another's. We need to know whether to use the printed word, some other kind of visual display, another medium of presentation (aural, tactile or olfactory), or a combination of media. We need to learn to understand the determinants of comprehension and retention, and to put that understanding into practice in the *creation* of the communications that will be seen as printed words, graphic designs, numbers, and so on. We need to learn how information should be presented for the most rapid and most accurate assimilation. We especially need to develop understanding of the requirements for on-the-spot use of professional information, as opposed to those that obtain in more traditional situations. In other words, we need to learn a great deal more about how the human brain processes information if we are to improve the ways in which we create and transmit intelligence. We refer here to the human engineering of communication. Our current knowledge of how to provide this is quite limited, which is regrettable. However, we almost never put what knowledge we do have to practical use, and that is inexcusable (see also Patricia Wright's papers in this volume).

There is another human side to communication, though, and this is also one that the technology enthusiasts tend to minimize or ignore. There is an important aesthetic dimension to the printed word (see, for example, Bailey, 1977) that is probably quite closely linked to the human factors I have already mentioned. The palpable devotion and artistry one sees in an Illuminated manuscript are necessarily absent from a photo-composed page, but there are other ways of providing aesthetic values that are not incompatible with modern technology. Good typography and design are, despite all appearances to the contrary, eminently possible with modern technology. There is a definite and growing commitment on the part of a number of enlightened users of new technology to seeing that the highest aesthetic standards are provided through their printed work. In the US, a typographic manifesto has been circulated among members of the Association of American University Presses (Kachergis, 1978); a well-known mathematician and computer scientist (Knuth, 1979) has developed an exciting new system for the computerized typesetting of mathematics and creation of fonts, simply because he cares about the appearance of his work; the Research and Engineering Council of the Graphic Arts Industry has established a Techno/Design Committee. These all provide evidence of the abiding interest which thoughtful persons have in retaining and enhancing human values in the material that the new technology is processing.

People in the entertainment industry use the computer term *software* with slightly altered meaning. For them, software is not the set of instructions that tell the equipment what to do; it is the program material itself (the musical performance on the gramophone record; the content of the video-cassette; and so on). In this frame of reference, we have been busy developing hardware without giving much thought to the software that will be disseminated through it. Our challenge, and what should be the most important development in future methods and techniques, will be to exploit the rapidly evolving hardware to present new and improved types of software — that is, to provide people with the information they want and need, at the proper time, in the proper form, wherever they need it. The creation and dissemination of the printed word will continue to be part art, part engineering. If we pursue it diligently and intelligently, we will improve the engineering and extend it into areas as yet barely touched on, and we will do so without losing the art. We may even advance it.

References

Argenti, J., *Systematic Corporate Planning*. Thomas Nelson and Sons, London, 1974.

Asimov, I., *Asimov's Guide to Science*. Basic Books, New York, 1972.

Bailey, H.S., Jr., The Traditional Book in the Electronic Age. The 1977 Bowker Memorial Lecture; reprinted in *Publishers Weekly*, 5 December 1977, p. 24-29.

Bell, D., *The Coming of Post-Industrial Society*. Basic Books, New York, 1973.

Kachergis, J., 'A Typographic Manifesto'. Unpublished document, 1978.

Knuth, D.E., *TEX, a System for Technical Text*. American Mathematical Society, 1979.

Price, D.J. de S, *Science Since Babylon*. Yale University Press, New Haven, Conn., 1961.

——, *Little Science, Big Science*. Columbia University Press, New York, 1963.

Rogers, E.M. and Shoemaker, F.F., *Communication of Innovations*, 2nd ed. Free Press, New York, 1971.

Steiner, G.A., *Top Management Planning*. Macmillan, London, 1969.

Strawhorn, J.M. et al., A Descriptive Model of Scientific and Technical Information Transfer. In: *Exploring Alternatives for the Expansion of the Access Improvement Program's Project on Innovation in Scientific Communication*. National Technical Information Service, 1977.

2. SOME QUESTIONS CONCERNING THE UNPRINTED WORD

MAURICE B. LINE
Director-General
British Library Lending Division,
Boston Spa, UK

The death of the printed word has been forecast for some years now. The reasoning behind these forecasts is clear enough: printing, paper and other publication costs are rising, while the costs of electronic storage and access are falling. The technology for storing large quantities of information compactly and retrieving it electronically over any distance is already here; it requires only that the present economic trends persist a few more years for the vision to become a reality.

Before we allow technology to change communication, we should first consider whether we want this to happen. What kind of future is promised for us? The attractions offered sound tempting. No longer need authors write or type their works on paper: they can key them straight into an electronic store. In time, they will not even need to do that, as there will be machines that will recognize speech patterns. Referees, editors and publishers will comment and edit on the text as displayed on their screens, and authors can amend their writing as necessary: the production of revised editions of works will be simple, so simple that works can if desired be subjected to more or less continuous revision. Would-be readers can ask their friendly computers what is available in a new field of interest or what is new in an established field of interest; they can call up abstracts instantly, followed by full text if wished. They can build up their personal 'libraries' of interesting and relevant works in compact stores, which can be easily weeded as desired. Gone will be space-consuming libraries, institutional and personal; gone will be the present physical barriers to world-wide communications.

As well as personal microcomputers and 'microlibraries', information will be accessible through television sets, which are especially well suited to pictorial matter and entertainment material such as plays and operas, as well as to the sort of information currently available through directories, encyclopedias and dictionaries. The coffee-table book, the reference work and the research paper will alike yield to the electronic revolution.

The effect on work will be great. Travel will become almost unnecessary. Conferences will take place on line; much office and administrative work will be done at home. Most of the manual work will of course be automated, so that management will become system management rather than man management.

All these things will be possible, but are they inevitable or desirable? Few would argue that none of them is inevitable or desirable. Economics will undoubtedly force some changes, and factors such as traffic congestion may well accelerate others such as the remote electronic office. More specifically, publication in conventional form is a grossly inappropriate, uneconomic and inefficient way of storing and making available research papers on topics of interest to perhaps ten or twenty people — and a considerable proportion of papers come within this category. The present procedures of searching bibliographic databases for relevant references and then having to request large numbers of papers on interlibrary loan, half of which prove on examination to be of no use for the purpose in question, suit no one.

At the other extreme there is no inevitability about popular novels, biographies or travel books. They continue to flourish, and to find a ready market even in difficult economic conditions. If they cease to be viable in conventional form, it is a safe bet that they will not be viable in electronic form. Nor is there any inevitability about textbooks, or even about many scholarly monographs, most of which presumably make a profit at present — this must be the assumption when new titles continue to appear at an undiminished rate. It is true that some publishers have been saying 'We have just managed to keep going up to now, but we are on the verge of collapse', but equally true that they have been saying this for some years. It is also true that some *have* collapsed, but publishing has always had a high failure rate, and there are few signs that it is getting any worse. Monographs with a small market — less than 1,000 — that might have been 'carried' on the backs of profitable titles a decade ago present a more difficult case, but there are methods of short-run publishing that seem able to produce editions as small as 500 without the publisher incurring a loss (for example the Royal Historical Society's "Studies in History" series), and there is also the possibility of on-demand publication from microform of camera-ready typescript.

The most obvious candidates for electronic storage are scholarly journal articles. However, journals containing a high proportion of articles in heavy demand are flourishing, and there seems to be no reason why they should not continue to do so. While some journals are undoubtedly experiencing difficulty in continuing publication, even when some of their costs are 'hidden' (because overheads are carried by academic institutions, editors are unpaid, and so on), many are making large profits and have a large enough market to ensure their continuance even if their costs rise much higher than they are at present. If these journals could be trimmed, perhaps by half, by cutting out articles that were in little demand, their future in conventional form would be even more fully assured.

In any case, it is not a question of choice between conventional and electronic modes. There are several points between, notably synopsis publication, whereby synopses of articles are published conventionally, and full texts are available on demand. This has the advantage that decisions on full text publication of papers can be made either initially or later, if demand reaches a certain level. At present the decision to publish an article is made according to whether it is a valid and significant contribution to the literature; referees and editors do not attempt to assess the size of readership, as book publishers must. With synopsis publication, the readership could be measured empirically. The quality of full text journals could thus be greatly improved, and with it their viability.

It seems then that a transition to electronic storage and access is economically inevitable only for a limited range of documents, chiefly research papers with a small readership. Assuming that it is more desirable to make something available in a different form, even if it is in some ways less satisfactory than the present form, than not to make it available at all, the question of desirability can be confined to those materials for which change is not economically inevitable.

An objective may be technically undesirable, socially or politically undesirable, or individually undesirable. Technically undesirable would be the prospect of a total breakdown of access as a result of computer failure. The breakdown might be only temporary — in any case replication of the database would be essential for reasons of security — and delay in retrieving desired information might be no longer than now, but in the electronic future there would be increased dependence on immediate access, for example in medicine. Delays may also occur because not all information can be held on line.

Electronic media require machines — computer terminals or television sets — for their use. These are by no means universally available at present, and even if their distribution were to be multiplied by a factor of twenty or even fifty over the next decade or two, huge numbers of the world's population would not have access to them. It could be argued that this applies at present to printed matter, but books can and do find their way into remote places, and, more important, there are no such barriers to the total spread of books as there are to electronic access media. The prospect that most information will be accessible only to an elite is surely very undesirable socially, and also politically in any democratic country. Moreover, control over access can be much more complete than with printed media; the dangers of abuse of this control for political or other purposes are obvious. There will be no *samizdat* in a totally electronic system.

One solution to the problem of restricted access within countries would be to produce something resembling conventional printed matter from the databases. If this is the *main* use to which some stored materials are put, however, the new media would merely be used as a means of producing old media. It looks in any case as if conventional publications will increasingly at some stage in their production be held in machine-readable form, so that what is under discussion is the end product, not the means of production.

Whether electronic access is *individually* desirable is a question that cannot be answered fully unless some other more fundamental questions are answered first. One problem is that it is not easy to distinguish the wishes and habits of people, which can be changed, from their basic needs, which cannot. In any case, remodelling users to fit systems is not a very attractive procedure. Undoubtedly there are some advantages in electronic access for the individual: instant access to vast stores of information and complete up-to-dateness, for example. However, there are equally obvious disadvantages. The first is that, as noted above, some machinery is necessary to use the system. Since most people do not do most of their reading near a computer terminal, this is a very severe limitation. Admittedly, if professional travel is going to be greatly reduced the amount of reading on trains and elsewhere away from offices will have to diminish, but this prospect raises a new set of questions as to whether people really want to stay more or less in one place most of the time. The space limitation could however be reduced or even abolished by the development of truly portable machines on which previously retrieved and stored information could be read.

A second disadvantage is more fundamental. A computer screen will hold only a fairly small number of words, and those in a form that is less easy and pleasant to read than the printed page. Leaving aside the question of readability — a by no means insignificant question if any time is spent reading — this limited display must have a profound effect on the way an article (or book) is read, on the speed of reading or scanning, and on comprehension. It seems likely that few people read an article in a linear fashion, from beginning to end; they may read the first paragraph or two to find out what it is about, and next possibly the conclusion; they may then scan the paper for diagrams, tables, or particular sections of relevance to them. This whole procedure may take only five or ten minutes, and may prove to be quite adequate; if not, the article may then, and only then, be read right through. If the same procedure were possible with electronic access — and there is no theoretical reason why articles should not be organized in different ways for a quite different medium — it would take much longer, because the visual span possible at one time is much more restricted. Evidence for this can be provided by everyday experience with a newspaper. This can be scanned, and the most relevant pieces identified, very quickly; the same process if only a screen-sized portion could be seen at any one time would take a very long time, even if pieces of potential relevance (a rather tricky concept) could be selected automatically.

There are other disadvantages. Researchers in many disciplines want or need to use two or more documents side by side: easy with books, difficult with electronic access unless printouts are obtained.

Some of the above disadvantages — an unpleasant visual medium, limited screen size, and the need for a machine to read the material at all — are shared by microforms. The fact that, after several decades, microforms are still disliked by the great majority of readers suggests that the computer or television screen may be no more acceptable as a medium for reading. It may of course be possible to have the best of both worlds: electronic access to documents which can be printed out in more or less conventional form for subsequent perusal if they are likely to deserve or require it. The electronic world need not supersede the conventional world: the option of producing the printed word will remain open. This applies not merely to individual papers printed out for individual use, but, as pointed out above, to whole journals. Nevertheless, the system will almost certainly be biased toward conventional or toward electronic access, because the costs of production in either form will make it difficult to maintain markets in both. Options *can* be left open; whether they *will* is another matter, one that should not be decided until much more is known about how people actually read articles or books.

Whether electronic or conventional access is appropriate — or for that matter microforms, synopses, or other 'intermediate' media — depends on various factors, as follows:

The *nature* of the material:
  its size,
  its subjects,
  its characteristics:

numerical, verbal, pictorial, etc.
descriptive, conceptual, experimental, historical, inter-
pretative, etc.
its style (discursive, concise)
its 'life' (archival, ephemeral, etc.);

The *audience* or *readership* (actual or intended):
its size
its nature (researchers, 'practitioners', 'common readers');

The *use* made of the material:
speed of access required
continuity of use
frequency of use
extent of use over time (permanence)
precision of access attainable (relevant to browsing need)
location of use
use in isolation or with other matter.

Economic data to which rapid and brief access is required are
ideally suited to electronic storage. At the other extreme, long
books requiring continuous reading, aimed at a large audience
and wide exposure, and containing important illustrations —
say, a comprehensive history of architecture — are equally
ideally suited to conventional publication (though an even
better form might be a book accompanied by a videocassette
for the illustrations). By analysing and categorizing documents
in some such way as suggested above, it is easy to define the
medium most suited to the majority of them. It is probable that
most *types* of documents (though possibly not the majority of
individual documents, as scientific and technical papers with a
small readership account for a high proportion of all published
items) would prove best suited to media not very different from
the familiar book. Such an analysis would be an extremely useful exercise. It would also demonstrate the great range of
material that is at present published; many technological prophets seem to assume that most (if not all) scholarly documents
are scientific papers.

If it proves that different matter requires different media —
and it would be very surprising if this conclusion were not

reached — the future system of storage and access will be a mixed one. Or rather, it *should* be: one reason why a serious attempt should be made to match media to matter is that we can then deliberately plan the future rather than watch misguided if well-intentioned technologists plan it for us. It ought to be a better future: technology should be seen as extending the range of media, and it would be a tragedy if instead it happened to restrict it.

What then of the future of the printed word? The future of the *existing* printed word — billions of billions of printed words — must not be forgotten. With advanced optical character recognition (OCR) techniques and computer input microfilm, it will be technically possible to convert most if not all existing printed works to electronic form. This could be done by identifying the documents most suited to this process (on the grounds of audience, usage, permanent interest, characteristics and so on) — papers on descriptive botany and zoology would be obvious candidates. There would seem little point in converting much printed material, at least unless and until the cost of storing and conserving it becomes much greater than the cost of conversion and subsequent access. The medium does affect the message, and Newton and Hobbes, not to mention Milton and Blake, thought in terms of ink on paper, not online terminals. (Indeed, it is also surprising how different it feels to read Milton and Hobbes in seventeenth- and twentieth-century printed editions.)

If, as seems likely, conversion to some different form of storage than paper is eventually necessary for much older printed matter, the same will apply in due course to the future printed word. Thus, not only a mixed but a changing future can be envisaged. Many documents should, and probably will, continue to be published in more or less conventional form, some in full text, some in reduced form as synopses, some on paper and some in microform. They will exist alongside electronic media, from which most of them will eventually be produced. When the printed forms of documents fall below a certain low volume of usage, or when they decay physically, this will not matter because their electronic forms will be retained, so that in effect the printed word will revert to electronic form.

The printed word will then be a very important, perhaps a

dominating, medium for communication of most information, but for most documents it will be only a temporary form: the printed butterfly will emerge from its electronic chrysalis, but it will also return again to it in due time. The vast majority of documents will thus be stored in electronic (chrysalis) form, but the majority of those used at any given time will be in their printed (butterfly) form.

This is one possible scenario, strongly influenced by the wishes and hopes of the writer — strongly influenced also by his belief that if enough people want things to develop in a certain way, there is a very good chance of their doing so, while if they are apathetic or unperceptive, they deserve what they get.

References

D.W. King and N.K. Roderer, Electronic processes: a solution to the economic difficulties facing small journals. *Journal of Research Communication Studies*, 2 (1), November 1979, 39-53.

D.W. King and N.K. Roderer, *Systems analysis of scientific and technical communications in the United States: the electronic alternative to communication through paper-based journals.* Rickville, Md., King Research, 1978. (PB 281 847-851).

F.W. Lancaster, *Towards paperless information systems.* Academic Press, New York, 1978.

J. Senders, An on-line scientific journal. *Information Scientist*, 11 (1), March 1977, 3-9.

Papers on the synopsis journal by C. Oppenheim and S. Price, R. Millson, I.A. Williams, S.J. Teague and D. Barr. *Journal of Research Communication Studies*, 1 (4), October 1978, 305-333.

3. THE PLACE OF THE PRINTED WORD IN TEACHING AND LEARNING

P. J. HILLS
Director, Primary Communications
Research Centre,
University of Leicester, UK

Definitions

For the purposes of this discussion we shall restrict the view of the education process to that of interactions — interactions which take place between teacher and students, and those between student and the materials available to him. These latter interactions are fundamental, especially when considered in the light of today's accessibility of knowledge, and consequently should have a very important place when considering training students in the learning process. I am conscious that this definition of the teaching and learning process is restrictive; it could very easily be widened to include librarian and book-seller — those concerned with the provision of the printed word. However I must emphasize that it is deliberately restrictive since it is with the use of a variety of types of material rather than their supply, that I am concerned.

In this paper I am adopting the definition of the printed word as that of text, diagram or equation, those things which are physically impressed by the use of ink on paper and so on. Nor am I forgetting that the written word is intrinsically bound up with the spoken word, both being necessary adjuncts in the teaching and learning process.

Teaching and learning methods: the present situation

Formal teaching consists for the most part of a teacher standing up in front of a group of students and displaying facts and ideas

37

by means of the lecture. Other methods in current use include group and individual tutorials, laboratory practical work in the case of science subjects, and more recently language laboratories, the beginnings perhaps of self-teaching, for students.

Communication between teacher and student has been mainly one-way, the teacher being seen as disseminator of knowledge. Colleagues in the area of humanities will probably disagree with this analysis since subjects here are taught in a much more interactive way, with small-group discussion and individual tuition taking place between the teacher and the student. However, over the past twenty years or so, in all subjects there has been much more of a shift from the emphasis on the teaching process to an emphasis on the learning process and upon the needs of the learner. This, coupled with the advent of a variety of media, methods and techniques now available to aid the process, has compelled the teacher to become, in addition to his other tasks, a manager of resources.

Whereas the teacher can be seen to be in an overall managerial position in relation to the whole, the student can be seen as at the centre of a number of potential interactions, as summarized in Figure 1.

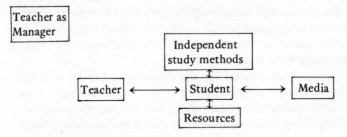

Figure 1. Teaching and learning interactions.

What part does the printed word play in these interactions? When considering it in relation to teacher-student interactions one can see that the teacher may supply printed notes for the student to keep for reference or suggest material which the student should find and read, either by buying the requisite book or journal or borrowing it from a library. In terms of student-media interactions, the printed word, when involved, serves to supply back-up or summary information, in the same way that printed notes or material gleaned from books serve as back-up in teacher-student interactions. *Media* in this particular context refers specifically to use of the blackboard or overhead projector by the teacher; display of visual material by slide, film or videotape; and perhaps to the use of music, speech and sounds on audio tape, all of which are used as display devices to pass information to the student.

Coming increasingly into use now are independent study methods which allow students to interact directly with structured schemes of work presented to them, often without the direct intervention of the teacher. This is perhaps the first step toward a fundamentally new approach to learning which is becoming increasingly necessary, as I shall show later. Many of these methods use a combination of printed materials, tape recordings and visual material, together with self-assessment tests and group sessions with other students and the teacher. For those who wish to explore the range of methods now available references have been given at the end of this paper (for example MacKenzie et al., 1976; Hills, 1980).

Independent study methods generally involve the student in working through a structured course with a virtually self-contained set of materials, and as a result small resource centres have been growing up in the US (Davis, 1971) and now in this country. These centres hold not only a variety of independent study materials but also a wide variety of other matter to which the student can be directed either as part of a course or as enrichment for it. A useful account of an integration of a library and resource centre for mainly non-printed materials is in Clarke (1976).

Because the programmed learning movement has played a part in the development of independent study methods we ought perhaps to have a brief look at its development. Up to this point in the discussion it has been assumed that in any reference to the printed word we were concerned with it in the form of traditional texts. In the 1960s the programmed learning movement produced a different kind of the printed word, mainly in the form of two types of programmed text, that of linear and multiple choice. These texts contained material which had been broken down into smaller units called 'frames', each frame basically containing some information and a question or a problem. Answers to these questions and problems were given to the student immediately an answer had been attempted so that the correctness or otherwise of the student's answer was confirmed or denied on the spot. Details of the types of strategy involved in writing such material are clearly described in a book by Susan Mayer Markle (Markle, 1969).

It was thought that programmed texts could thus fulfil the functions of a good teacher, that is, that as well as imparting the basic factual material of a course it would allow the student to practice what he or she had learned and, by working through the text in a structured sequential way, to build up ideas and concepts from simple factual beginnings.

Programmes were in the form of paper texts and in other forms such as photographic films which were held in a variety of devices which came to be known as 'teaching machines'. It is significant to note that the yearbook of the Association for Programmed Learning and Educational Technology recorded the availability of thirty such machines in 1969, only six in 1976, and has now decided to omit any mention of such machines from its pages. Although the programmed learning movement foundered on over-commercialization and the lack of suitable programmes for a diversity of teaching machines, the basic principles of programming were sound. These basic principles were those of active learning, that is, involving the student himself in his learning; feeding back information on progress; and promoting understanding by working from simple material to more complex ideas. Programmes printed on paper have continued to prove of use in limited situations, especially:

(1)   in providing simple introductions to subjects;
(2)   in allowing a student to work on his own to obtain the background information necessary for entry to a subject at a higher level;
(3)   for revision of a topic already known; and
(4)   in providing sequences of instructions, thus enabling the user to acquire skills in the use of equipment.

Whereas the printed word in normal text form puts the skills of interpretation and use on the reader, programmed material of this kind can help the reader by guiding his throught processes and thus actively promote learning.

At the present time our educational system is firmly paper-based, that is, the printed word is used both as a back-up medium for independent study and, of course, as a storage and retrieval system in the form of books held either in a student's collection or in a library. The advent of microcomputers, electronic data storage and retrieval, and data transmission systems may change this picture somewhat.

Implications for the future

The teacher no longer has to be the sole disseminator of all knowledge, because today to an even greater extent than in the past students are able to draw on information sources outside those available within the formal setting, that is, from the great variety of books available in libraries, from television programmes, and from radio and so on.

In addition to easy access to books and television, the student of the present day in all probability owns a record player, cassette tape recorder and pocket calculator, all of which are non-print media for the display of information. The present trend toward the availability of cheap microcomputers will continue and such devices are capable of displaying and manipulating text and graphics in a very powerful and interactive way.

There are two important implications here, one, a possible trend away from the formal educational setting — a building specifically set aside for the purposes of education where teachers teach and students learn — toward a more home-based educational system, the other, a possible minimization or elimination of the need for the printed word and for paper-based materials through use of equipment such as microcomputers, television, video and audio cassette recorders, which could provide interactive independent study courses.

Education without a formal setting

Let us consider the possibility of a trend away from education in a formal setting with a special building and people designated as teachers. Open University courses give some indication of what this would be like. In this particular instance it succeeds largely because it is concerned with adult learners, working mainly in their own homes, who are highly motivated to learn. However it must be noted that even here their work does not take place entirely at home, since there are a number of regional centres which they visit and at regular intervals they meet in groups at courses. A tutor is also assigned to them for help and advice; they are able to contact him whenever they need to. Thus, even though the Open University functions through what has been described as a multimedia home correspondence course, it does require contact with tutor-teachers and does require its students to meet in groups at intervals. It is also at present a system based to a great extent on the printed word — the course texts often being those used in other, more conventional, university courses.

The need for a formal setting for teaching and learning must also be considered in terms of the purposes of education. The purpose of education in a society is to transmit not only a basic knowledge and set of skills to its members, but also to pass on values and standards to the coming generation in order to safeguard the existence of the society. In a formal educational setting where students come together with teachers to pursue the purposes of education, then this basis of fact, information, values and standards can be given a framework in which they are not simply set but are displayed in a wide context of use. The teacher has a wider appreciation than the student holds initially. Therefore he is able to give guidance to the student in setting the facts in their true context, to show him how they have been used in other situations, give a personal approach to them, and to allow him to use them in practice in a controlled way. The one essential feature of a formal educational setting is that the students are assembled in one place, at one time, on a regular basis, together with their teacher; they can discuss problems, ideas, facts, opinions with each other, either in discussion groups or simply as part of the normal social interaction.

Mature students pursuing Open University or correspondence-type courses often complain of the sense of isolation. It would seem that interaction with students engaged on similar work is a necessary condition in the process of learning, even if this is only seen as the need to air one's knowledge and ideas and see how it is received by others. The above discussion assumes that the will to learn exists, since when one has reached the point of entry to a university or college that will should be strong.

The elimination of the need for the printed word

If teaching and learning were merely a transfer of information from teacher to student, then once the book arrived the teacher should have been dispensable as a major figure in the teaching and learning process; students should have been able to learn merely by recourse to suitable books read in their own homes. Why then has this not happened? This question has already in part been answered in terms of the need for students to meet their teachers and to be involved actively in discussion and practice instead of reading passively about a subject, although of course a certain amount of random reading should certainly be done.

The printed word can obviously go a long way toward making details of knowledge and skills available; it can put forward values and standards, at least from the writer's point of view. In the form of a normal text however it does little more than display the material, and therefore it is up to the student in what way he receives, interprets and uses this information.

This is where the programmed learning texts were thought to have advantages over conventional textual materials, since they involved the learner, gave him practice in using the material and supplied him with instant feedback on the correctness or otherwise of his answers. The fact that paper-based programmed texts were successful and teaching machines were not is indicative only of the over-commercialization forced upon the programmed learning movement and the relative crudity of the machines then in use. The microcomputer is potentially a very flexible teaching device and when its capacity for information storage and retrieval is allied to this it could become the teaching machine of the eighties. The microcomputer overcomes the disadvantages of cost, space and ease of use of the mainframe computer and will be used in educational settings for the kinds of things computers are already used for — information retrieval, information giving, problem solving, manipulation of mathematical models, simulation of different experiments and so on. Accounts of these and other possible uses will be found in Hooper and Toye (1975) and Rushby (1979). In education, the microcomputer, using programmed learning techniques, and with its capacity for interaction with the learner, could supplant or eliminate the paper-based programmed text if all students had easy access to it.

Even if microcomputers did not become as universally available as is thought probable, other important developments which carry a considerable implication for home-based education, seemingly without the need for the printed word, are data transmission systems like PRESTEL, CEEFAX and ORACLE. CEEFAX and ORACLE, the BBC and ITV data systems display information on the normal television screen without any possible interaction with the viewer. However, PRESTEL, the Post Office's system, is an interactive system and thus has many more possible implications for educational use. The viewer is able to 'call up' images on the screen by punching a combination of numbers on a keyboard and is able to select a variety of alternatives displayed on the screen. At worst this could be likened to the multiple-choice programmes of the original teaching-machine era. The educational implications of this system however have not yet been fully investigated. With the use of regional computer centres designed to increase the interactive component of this system on a local basis, it is likely that correspondence courses of the future could switch to such a system at the expense of present-day printed texts.

These electronic developments, both in the formal educational setting and for home-based learning, would seem virtually to eliminate the need for the printed word since they can supply text, diagrams and equations, and also offer an interactive element together with information storage and retrieval facilities, but without the personality of the book which is so aptly brought out by Heathorn (see "Learn with BOOK").

Implications for the future

Although this paper has looked at the teaching and learning process in relation to the printed word as a more or less conventional progression from situations which currently exist, we must bear in mind that the situation is in all probability not going to remain as simple as this. It may be necessary to take a radical jump in our thinking because of the speed of development not only in the technological field but also more importantly in the increase and spread of knowledge. In the very near future man will have to take account of vast quantities of knowledge, or sink. In the first paper John Strawhorn described the brain functioning as a limited capacity storage and retrieval system. It is increasingly being realized that as the amount of information grows and as it becomes more easily and quickly available there will be a need to teach individuals strategies for both dealing with information and for accessing quickly the information available.

Future courses may not be examined by testing the limits of an individual's memory but instead may challenge a student's strategies for obtaining information quickly, for ordering it into a logical sequence, for arriving at conclusions from given facts and for accurate and rapid problem solving. Nor is it necessary to wait for the new technology before this can happen. It may be necessary to have access to a computer database via a video-screen and terminal for full realization of the possibilities, but the strategies are available now and can be, indeed are being explored without the need of complex hardware.

We must however never lose sight of the need for the sound basis of learning upon which to build the individual's own thought processes. One cannot teach the uses of a calculator without having first taught the basic principles of mathematics, so in a wider context can this be applied to all knowledge. The broad purpose of education must be allied with the ability to abstract and cope with concepts and developments. Perhaps this is where the book can help!

References

Clarke, J., 'The Implications of Implementing Change for an Institution of Higher Education.' In *Aspects of Educational Technology*, volume X, Clarke, J. and Leedham, J., eds., Kogan Page, London, 1976.

Davis, H.S., *Instructional Media Centers*, Indiana University Press, Bloomington, 1971.

Hills, P.J., *The Self-Teaching Process in Higher Education*, Croom Helm, London, 1976.

Hills, P.J., Information Package on Teaching and Learning Methods for Librarians. BLRDD Report 5512, British Library, London, 1980.

Hooper, R. and Toye, I., *Computer Assisted Learning in the United Kingdom: Some Case Studies*, Council for Educational Technology, London, 1975.

MacKenzie, N., Eraut, M. and Jones, H.C., *Teaching and Learning: An Introduction to New Methods and Resources in Higher Education*, UNESCO, Paris, 1970.

Markle, S.M., *Good Frames and Bad: A Grammar of Frame Writing*, 2nd edition, John Wiley and Sons, New York, 1969.

Rushby, N.J., 'An Introduction to Educational Computing'. *New Patterns of Learning*, Hills, P.J., ed., Croom Helm, London, 1979.

4. THE DESIGN OF OFFICIAL INFORMATION I — GOBBLEDYGOOK?

PATRICIA WRIGHT
MRC Applied Psychology Unit,
15 Chaucer Road, Cambridge, UK

The domain of official information

Government departments, both local and central, frequently need to communicate with the general public. They advise the public on health and safety matters such as the dangers of smoking or the desirability of wearing seatbelts. They provide the public with information about numerous social services such as legal aid, welfare benefits, transportation services, customs regulations and so on. They also ask the public for information, not only in censuses and in tax returns, but whenever licences are applied for (for example marriage licences, vehicle licences). Indeed forms are part of almost every transaction between those executing government policy and the public who are administered.

At present these communications involve the printed word, although not necessarily as the sole means of communication. Posters on hoardings may be adjuncts to televised advertisements and leaflets all communicating essentially the same message. Similarly a printed leaflet explaining pension rights or national insurance contributions may need to be supplemented by a knowledgeable clerical officer who can answer questions and untangle confusions. Forms too may in some instances need the expertise of a third party if communication between public and officialdom is to be successful. There are numerous complaints about the difficulties of understanding official information (see Ryan, 1978; Hampson, 1978; Turner, 1980). Nevertheless print is well established as a major thread in the network of official information. Will this change with the advance of the new technology? Will print become the adjunct, the last resort, the safety net to other more modern ways of disseminating information? If it does, will gobbledygook become extinct?

One basis for evaluating the new technologies is to examine the principles which underlie the design of effective written communications. Research into information design has for the most part considered printed displays (see Tinker, 1965; Spencer, 1969; Hartley, 1978). It will therefore be necessary to consider to what extent the principles of designing printed communications so that they are easily understood will apply *mutatis mutandis* to soft-copy displays. A rather different approach to predicting the extinction of gobbledygook concerns the extent to which the new technologies themselves will be able to offer a sophisticated design tool for improving printed information. The old and the new technologies can be seen not only as rivals but as mutually supportive. For example, electronic hardware and software both require documentation, but can be recruited as producers of such printed copy (see Frase, 1979).

Although the following discussion will focus on communications involving the general public, it is of course realized that government departments also have numerous interactions with professional groups such as lawyers and medical personnel, town planners and industrial organizations. The decision to exclude such communications from the present paper was made not because they are of little account, nor because they will be unaffected by technological developments, but simply because they raise certain special issues about communication which do not apply to information directed at the public. For example, there is not space here to explore fully issues such as training people to use specialized information resources (such as computer-aided design in town planning departments) or specialized communication techniques (such as computerized word-processing systems). Nevertheless many of the points which will be made about designing information so that it can be readily used will apply in principle to the information displays used by professional groups.

The information made available by government departments

for the general public tends to reach two rather different target audiences. On the one hand there is some information which tends to be (actively) sought by the public, for example details of a fuel rebate scheme. On the other hand there is information which the government feels obliged to provide even though the public is not particularly keen to receive it, for example health advice. Table 1 shows how various kinds of written materials mentioned earlier fall into categories with respect to who is asking for the information.

Table 1. Who wants to know what: the public's interaction with different kinds of official information.

	Tell	Ask
Government	advertising (health and safety)	forms (income, driving)
Public		leaflets, display boards (benefits, travel information)

Again it seems necessary to narrow the domain of written information to be considered in what follows. Advertising is in a number of respects different from the other media, for example its message is seldom cognitively complex. In contrast, understanding forms and leaflets can at times require some fairly agile mental gymnastics. Another important difference between the 'telling' and 'asking' columns of the table is that the advantages of the interactive facility which can be provided by computerized interrogation appear less relevant to the advertising media. Consequently the domain of official information which will be considered here in detail will centre around the three areas of forms, leaflets and travel information. In their conventional printed mode, forms and leaflets are hand-held, viewed at normal reading distance and, to varying extents, prose-like. In contrast, travel information is often wall-mounted and viewed from a distance; examples are the departure times at bus and railway stations, diversion signs along the highway or directional information within building complexes. One of the common characteristics of most travel information is that extended prose is seldom involved. Figure 1 (p. 60) is perhaps the exception rather than the rule, but it illustrates the kind of communication that might well be simpler for the reader if electronics were used to display only the information relevant for the current time of day.

It is true that travel information is not always 'printed' on paper, but its inclusion here is particularly convenient because it provides a way of examining the extent to which a design approach that gives rise to effectively structured dialogues between the public and the printed page is likely to generate design heuristics that apply in other contexts where the public is interrogating visually displayed information.

Before examining the design issues within each of these domains it would be appropriate to consider some of the more general issues relating to the design of visual displays. This more general discussion will help to set the scene for evaluating the impact of alternative ways of providing the public with official information.

Some principles of information design

There are two starting points from which one can consider the problems of information design. These correspond to the rather different viewpoints of writers and readers. For example, one can begin with the originators of the message, analyse the message's intrinsic structure and major objectives and on the basis of such an analysis first select the presentation medium and then make further design decisions within the chosen display mode. Alternatively one can focus on readers, on how they will be using the information, what they will be looking for, what questions they will have in mind, and so on. Of these two approaches, the writer- or text-based approach is generally the easier to adopt. It is relatively straightforward to specify the objectives of the communication. Thereafter, economic considerations can motivate the selection of medium and other design options. This is a design strategy adopted by many organizations, both inside and outside government. Not all such organizations have made a conscious decision between the alternatives, but it may just seem a natural starting point for writers to begin with what they want to say.

However, paying so little heed to readers can run certain risks. Perhaps the most serious of these is the risk that the information will not be read at all. Just as the manufacturers of equipment complain that members of the public do not read the operating instructions carefully enough, so the producers of forms complain that the public does not give enough attention to the notes which explain the precise meanings of particular questions. It is worth asking if this behaviour is the reader's 'fault', if he is any more to blame than he would be for not having the three hands needed for some self-assembly furniture. If the general public have certain predictable characteristics in their patterns of reading then it might be more fruitful to adopt the ergonomic approach of adapting the information environment to the reader's requirements and limitations. The alternative Procrustean hope that in time readers will learn to behave the way that writers want inevitably generates a great deal of frustration and annoyance among consumers in the short term without any guarantee of success in the longer term.

Basing design decisions on an analysis of readers' behaviour requires an understanding of what is known about the process of reading. First it must be emphasized that there is no single process, or even system of processes, which corresponds to 'reading'. For example, Sticht (1977) has differentiated between 'reading-to-do' and 'reading-to-learn'. The first of these applies to the reading of a set of instructions, the second would refer to material such as the highway code and also to the more traditional activity of reading for comprehension. Even here, when reading for comprehension, it has been found that readers who are trying to get an overview of the argument tend to adopt different reading strategies, as indicated by their speed of reading and the distribution of their pauses, from those who are trying to remember specific details (Samuels and Dahl, 1975). This notion of strategy selection by readers has important consequences for the design of written information. In particular it emphasizes that readers are not necessarily starting in the top left-hand corner and progressing in a steady linear fashion to the end of the text (Wright, 1979a). Readers' desire to move both backwards and forwards through a text such as a leaflet may be one aspect of reading that will be less easily accommodated in the new technologies, which are discussed in the next paper.

The snag about trying to design information from the starting point of reader strategies is that it resembles trying to build on sand. There are so many strategies that readers can adopt for a particular text (see Olshavsky, 1976-1977) that there is a need for finding some stepping-stones through the quagmire. One possible solution comes from the suggestion by Wright (1979b) that the interaction between a reader and a text can be analysed in terms of its cognitive components. For different texts or different target populations or different reading objectives the set of relevant components may vary. Nevertheless, by focussing upon these constituents it becomes possible to introduce consideration of the 'human factors' elements into decisions about design options. This will be illustrated in more detail a little later for specific kinds of official information. For the present it may suffice to consider in general terms what cognitive processes are drawn upon during reading and what implications these have for design decisions.

At its simplest, reading must involve three classes of cognitive factors which can be loosely labelled as perceptual, linguistic, and decision or response processes. The perceptual factors are often thought to refer only to the legibility of the material. Legibility is obviously important, but the perceptual processing undertaken by readers includes much more than simply word recognition. Waller (1979) has pointed out that typographic variation within the material is a valuable way of helping readers find the information that they are seeking. Katzen (1979) has aptly referred to these directional guides as signposts. Such signposts for the printed word may include headings, indentations, marginal annotations, and so on. When considering the adequacy with which a different medium might replace the printed word it is therefore necessary to evaluate how effectively it can cater for the relevant perceptual processing that the reader will wish to undertake.

The linguistic factors which determine how easily the information can be understood and used can be subdivided into factors relating to words, sentences and paragraphs. A change of presentation medium is unlikely to have much effect on the comprehension of words, except for people with relatively low-level literacy skills where an auditory presentation may be valuable. However, for the most part the problems that the public face in understanding the words within official communications arise because the writer is using jargon terms or archaic expressions (Wright, 1978). Such problems will not disappear when this same information is displayed on a television screen. Similarly at the sentence level, convoluted syntax will remain incomprehensible no matter in what visual medium it is displayed. At the paragraph level and above, that is whenever it is necessary for the reader to grasp the cohesive thread of a lengthy passage, then there may be important differences between turning the pages of a booklet and scrolling through screenfuls of text. In particular the decisions about where the 'page' should end, decisions which writers often leave for printers, may be much more critical for electronic presentations.

The notion that readers are frequently making decisions and other responses when they read is not well established either in reading research or in information design, but it has been pointed out that readers frequently ask themselves questions such as "Do I already know this?" or " Did I want to know this?". Depending on the answers readers reach, so will their reading strategy vary. The notion of readers taking decisions or responding to text is more self-evident when the text is itself a precursor to some immediate action, as it is for example in much of the information provided for travellers (timetables, departure gates and so on) and also in information leaflets explaining to householders about saving energy or surviving nuclear attack. Here the general assessments of 'readability' or 'comprehensibility' can have serious shortcomings and alternative notions of 'usability' may need to be developed to give adequate scope for assessing the referential interpretation of the message. To cite a fairly trivial example of a text which is easily understood but whose message is uninterpretable, in our office we have a photocopying maching that carries the message 'To restart, press the green reset button'. There would seem to be no comprehension problems here, but unfortunately the green button is nowhere in sight. Indeed it is found under a hinged metal lid which can only be raised if part of the equipment on top of it is pushed to one side. Similar denotative problems can arise with official information. This is another reason why it can be ultimately more satisfactory in terms of effective communication, albeit inherently more difficult, to focus information design on the needs of the user rather than on the message of the writer.

Having briefly indicated some of the psychological processes which determine the success of a reader's interaction with textual information it would seem appropriate to outline in general terms what impact new technologies might have on the success of these communications. One of the most obvious points when thinking of many CRT displays is that the range of typographic variation is much less than is available for print. For example even common distinctions such as italic and boldface fonts are seldom available. If the information on the CRT is wanted in hard copy form then the reader can have the printout in any colour he likes as long as it is black! CRT displays tend to mean that the maximum page size is one of the constraints within which the information must be designed. In contrast Hartley (1978) has argued that determining the appropriate page size for a document should be one of the decisions made early in the design process. Clever foldings, which can serve a number of functions in printed leaflets, require quite different design solutions for the CRT screen, perhaps incorporating some of the split-screen techniques advocated by Teitelman (1979).

It is not the intention to pour cold water on the potential of the new technologies — far from it. They can provide some very neat solutions to the limitations of the printed word. Nevertheless some of the limitations of the new technologies have been mentioned before discussing some of their advantages because it is, understandably, the potential benefits that we hear most about from the manufacturers.

Certainly there will be a range of design options opened up

by computer-based display facilities which do not seem to be viable for print on paper. For example, at present the dissemination of information about welfare benefits is primarily done through leaflets. Typically a leaflet will concentrate on one specific benefit and deal with the sub-categories of people who are entitled to claim that benefit. This is clearly a significant writing strategy from an administrative viewpoint since the benefit will be administered from some specific geographic location (such as the town hall). At these locations officials will have to deal with varieties of claimants. However, from the public's point of view it is less obvious whether this is the most useful way of organizing welfare information. One alternative would be to have material that addressed particular sections of the public, such as pensioners or single-parent families. Such leaflets could explain the range of benefits to which this section of the community was entitled. In print, this user-based organization can mean a lot of expensive duplication of information in different leaflets. However, interactive computer facilities may enable individuals to have written information structured in the way that they prefer. This in turn may reduce the amount of irrelevant information with which the reader has to deal. Yet such advantages may need to be weighed against the potential snags that may arise with the new technology. Some of these disadvantages will become clearer as specific kinds of official information are considered in more detail below, but it is possible that in addition to 'bureaucratic gobbledygook' there are risks of 'technological gobbledygook' and 'display gobbledygook' increasing the public's problems in understanding official communications.

Some factors relating to the selection of information media

An analysis of information users can indicate where print on paper has shortcomings, and by so doing it can point to areas where innovations would be most welcome. This approach to information design can be equally applicable to information presented in any medium. Indeed many of the research findings indicating display factors which are highly desirable for print will apply straightforwardly to other kinds of display. Nevertheless it is pertinent to raise a number of questions about display innovations. For example: Where are they most needed? What sorts of information would be best transferred from print to other media? How does the information provider choose the medium for presenting a particular message?

Few of these questions have been addressed by behavioural researchers. Indeed even mundane distinctions such as when is it better to listen than to read have usually been explored only with prose-like materials (e.g. Horowitz and Berkowitz, 1967), whereas, given that there are adults with underdeveloped literacy skills, the elderly with relatively poor visual acuity, and non-native speakers of English for whom reading is a hurdle, it might well be feasible to make the *a priori* case that for disseminating official information both visual and auditory modes are necessary. It remains to be established whether the individual at a computer-controlled terminal should be assailed by ear and eye simultaneously or whether there should initially be a choice of presentation mode. As yet few of the logistic problems such as backtracking or remembering multiple-choice options appear to have been explored for auditory presentation. Nevertheless in the realm of official information the target audience very often includes those who have difficulty in reading, for one reason or another, so help such as REPEAT buttons may be very necessary.

The popularity of interactive television games might lead one to think that the physical characteristics of the hardware of the new technologies will not be off-putting to the potential user. However this impression may be derived from and apply to the young much more than to the elderly. Among the latter there remain people who have never used a telephone, who are frightened of lifts and who do not have a kitchen cluttered with labour-saving gadgets. The proportion of the population falling into this category will presumably decrease in time, nevertheless this proportion is always likely to contain some of the economically most disadvantaged groups which are the target audience for many official communications. Where the cognoscenti are happy to ask playful questions such as, 'What will happen if I press this button?' the diffident are more likely to be beset with questions such as 'Will it bite?', 'Will it break?', 'Will I have to pay for it?'

Related to the question of which sections of the public will find it comfortable to use the new technologies is the issue of the amount of documentation which accompanies each installation. Powerful systems provide their users with a lot of options, but not knowing how to exploit these options can be a serious problem. Computer documentation has a track record even worse than official information. If you have to learn a completely new language in order to take your PET for a walk then alternative systems of string and sealing wax may seem to have a great deal in their favour. The operation of many of the new systems such as PRESTEL and CEFAX requires the consultation of instruction booklets. Anyone who thought that the electronic media might replace the printed word has simply not looked at the total package on display in any computer department. Moreover the numerous horror stories associated with computer documentation that is systems-oriented rather than user-oriented should serve as a cautionary tale for innovations intended for use by the public. It has been reported that over 92 per cent of computer users in one survey were not prepared to read system manuals, and 60 per cent would not read the four-page manual which provided the minimal instruction for using the system (Williams, 1977). Some computer companies now make it one of their selling points that their documentation is comprehensible. Perhaps it is not already too late.

Associated with this point are the general ergonomic issues of control and display functions. Buttons need to be marked unambiguously and grouped functionally in relation to the display (see Stewart, 1976; Moore, 1976). For example if a screen is used in scrolling mode and the forward and backward buttons are vertically aligned it probably maps onto people's stereotypes more easily if the button labelled 'Next page' is underneath the button labelled 'Previous page'. It is interesting to note that in this context the use of arrows as button labels seems to become highly ambiguous. The 'Next page' arrow could be pointing upwards, which is the notional direction in which the present page will move, or pointing downwards if the reader thinks of his own need as being a wish to move downwards. Perhaps the public, as yet unaccustomed to the characteristics of continuous stationery, does not think in these terms at all, but in the conventional left-to-right pagination of the printed page. The advantages of trying to determine how the user thinks about and internally represents the problem have been emphasized in a number of other places (e.g. Barnard et al., 1977).

One final point that must be taken into account when evaluating the pros and cons of transferring from print to a new medium is the reliability of the new technology. The salesman will emphasize the joys of having up-to-date information at one's fingertips. The reality may be that there is no information at all for a couple of days because the machine has developed a fault and the engineer cannot come until tomorrow. Some indication of how serious a factor this can be, apropos of interactive information displays being used by the public, is given by a visit to the human biology exhibition in the British Museum of Natural History in London. Undoubtedly the exhibits have much to contend with in terms of rough handling by young and inexperienced users. Nevertheless there was a disappointingly high proportion of non-functioning displays on my last visit. Clearly there are two separable components of the speed of accessing information. One component relates to the ease of getting into a position of being able to interact with a database, whether electronic or printed; the second relates to the subsequent speed of retrieving the required information. Interactive electronic systems may have many advantages relative to print, as far as the second of these components is concerned, but there is still a degree of uncertainty surrounding the first component. Doubtless in time this will disappear just as the television interludes, and cards assuring the public that normal service will be resumed as soon as possible, are historic relics of an emerging technology. In the short term the fallibility of the hardware may itself be an argument for having available printed information at least as a back-up system.

References

Barnard, P., Morton, J., Long, J. and Ottley, P.: Planning menus for display: some effects of their structure and content on user performance. In *Displays for Man-Machine Systems*. Institute of Electrical Engineers Conference Publication No. 150, p. 130-133, 1977.

Frase, L.T.: The problem of multiple markets and evolving product lines for Bell System documentation. Report available from the author at Bell Laboratories, Piscataway, N.J., USA, 1979.

Hampson, R.: A study of DHSS leaflets: the language of bureaucracy. Report available from the author at the Department of Social Administration, University of Bristol, UK, 1978.

Hartley, J.: *Designing Instructional Text*. London: Kogan Page, 1978.

Horowitz, M.W. and Berkowitz, A.: Listening and reading, speaking and writing: an experimental investigation of differential acquisition and reproduction of memory. *Perceptual and Motor Skills, 24,* 207-215, 1967.

Katzen, M.: Quoted in "Designing information: some approaches, some problems and some suggestions." British Library Research and Development Department Report No. 5509, 1979.

Moore, T.G.: Controls and tactile displays. In K.F. Kraiss and J. Moraal (eds.), *Introduction to Human Engineering*. Cologne: TUV Rheinland, 1976.

Olshavsky, J.E.: Reading as problem solving: an investigation of strategies. *Reading Research Quarterly, 12,* 654-674, 1976-1977.

Ryan, R.: Britain — a nation of form-fillers. *Cambridge Evening News,* 14 September, 1978.

Samuels, S.J. and Dahl, P.R.: Establishing appropriate purposes for reading and its effect on flexibility of reading rate. *Journal of Educational Psychology, 67,* 38-43, 1975.

Spencer, H.: *The Visible Word*. London: Lund Humphries, 1969.

Stewart, T.F.M.: Displays and the software interface. *Applied Ergonomics, 7,* 137-146, 1976.

Sticht, T.G.: Comprehending reading at work.
In M.A. Just and P.A. Carpenter (eds.), *Cognitive Processes in Comprehension*. Hillsdale, N.J.: Lawrence Erlbaum Associates, 1977.

Teitelman, W.: A display oriented programmer's assistant. *International Journal of Man-Machine Studies, 11,* 157-187, 1979.

Tinker, M.A.: *The Legibility of Print*. Ames: Iowa State University Press, 1965.

Turner, F.: Fighting forms. *'She'*, p. 72, February 1980.

Waller, R.: Typographic access structures for educational texts. In P.A. Kolers, M.E. Wrolstad and H. Bouma (eds.), *Processing of Visible Language*, 1. New York: Plenum Press, 1979.

Williams, P.W.: Quoted in *New Scientist*, 76, 769, 22/29 December, 1977.

Wright, P.: "Is legal jargon a restrictive practice?" Paper presented at the SSRC Law and Psychology Seminar Group Meeting, Oxford, 1980. Proceedings to be edited by S. Lloyd-Bostock and published by Macmillan under the title *Psychology in Legal Contexts: Applications and Limitations*.

Wright, P.: "Textual literacy: an outline sketch of psychological research on reading and writing." Paper presented at the NATO conference on *Processing Visible Language*, 2, Toronto, 1980a. Proceedings to be edited by P.A. Kolers, M.E. Wrolstad and H. Bouma and published by Plenum Press, New York, 1979a.

Wright, P.: "Usability: the criterion for designing written information." Paper presented at the NATO conference on *Processing Visible Language*, 2, Toronto, 1980b. Proceedings to be edited by P.A. Kolers, M.E. Wrolstad and H. Bouma and published by Plenum Press, New York.

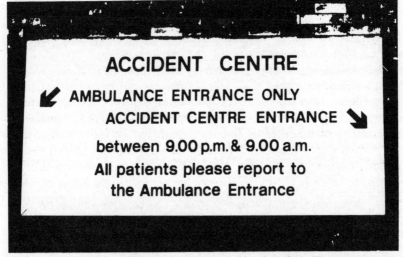

Figure 1. This notice, displayed at a Cambridge hospital, illustrates some of the complexities people face when following directions.

5. THE DESIGN OF OFFICIAL INFORMATION II – THE NEW TECHNOLOGIES

PATRICIA WRIGHT
MRC Applied Psychology Unit,
15 Chaucer Road, Cambridge, UK.

The objective of this paper is to discuss forms, leaflets and travel information in relation to what the users of these are doing while they interact with them, and to indicate what implications there are in this for design decisions.

Forms

Interrogation by a computer is not necessarily an unpleasant affair. When a computer in a Glasgow hospital was programmed to collect case-history data from patients several people reported that it seemed more 'human' than the usual interaction with medical personnel. Another advantage of responding to such a dialogue rather than filling in a piece of paper is that the form-filler can have feedback about the answers. For example someone applying for a welfare benefit could have an instant assessment of whether or not they qualified, or indeed whether they might be financially better off applying for a different benefit (Adler and du Feu, 1975). The same can be true when inquiring about travel facilities, for example making airline reservations or booking a package holiday, but here there is usually a human intermediary between the computer and the form-filler. This hybrid of form-filler plus expert plus computer may be only a temporary feature of the system, although, if linked through developments such as the videophone (see Dickson and Bowers, 1973), this combination might have a number of advantages both over the present system and over a fully automatic one. In comparison with the present system of either

61

making mistakes because the form has been misunderstood or making a special journey to obtain expert advice, the advantages are obvious. In comparison with fully automatic systems the value of a human intermediary may lie in making the system available or acceptable to a broader section of the public and at the same time providing a combined visual and auditory presentation which could easily operate in only one modality if required (for example if the form-filler were either deaf or blind).

Although for economic reasons the ultimate objective may be a fully automated system of asking questions and collecting answers, it looks as though there may be several hybrid versions in operation before this stage is achieved (Brown, et al., 1979). Designing printed forms so that the answers can be electronically read is one hybrid which in some of its manifestations clearly reduces the usability of the information. For example some of the forms designed for optical mark reading can produce problems both of legibility and of response complexity (see Figure 1, p. 77).

In the analysis of design principles discussed previously, the broad spectrum of usability was subdivided into cognitive processes such as perceiving, comprehending and responding. We can ask what implications such an analysis has for forms? This may indicate how similar will be the design considerations for print and other media.

Perceiving
The perceptual problems for printed forms are threefold. Firstly the form-filler needs to be able to perceive the overall path through the form. Some questions may follow each other vertically down the page; others may run in a horizontal formation across the page. It is easy on some forms to omit questions inadvertently because the route through the form is far from clear. When the form is presented on a television screen then it may be practicable to deal with just one question at a time, thus circumventing the problem of routing the form-filler from one question to the next. In particular, computer-based query systems may often be able to route form-fillers through only the relevant questions. There have been serious attempts

attempts to get branching structures or 'jump-questions' onto printed forms since the idea was illustrated by Jones (in 1968) (for example if the answer to question 3 is yes then the form-filler continues with question 4, whereas if the answer is no then he is instructed to jump to question 8). Computer-based question and answer techniques would seem to offer ideal solutions.

The second perceptual problem posed by forms concerns the legibility of the question itself. Here print, with its ready availability of well-formed lowercase letters may often have advantages over CRT displays restricted to capitals, or to an artificial typeface, and often subject to problems of glare and flicker (Hultgren and Knave, 1974). Where only a single question at a time is being displayed, then the CRT should be able to provide much more space than is practicable on the printed page. This space can be used both for increasing the size of the typeface and for increasing the interline spacing. Both factors increase the ease with which the text can be read (Tinker, 1965). Perception can involve other sensory modalities besides vision. The effects of having simultaneous visual and auditory presentations have sometimes been found advantageous in the context of computer-assisted learning (see Atkinson, 1976). Certainly auditory presentation would be one way of increasing the independence of some sections of the community (such as the visually handicapped and the illiterate) who are unable to cope easily with written displays.

The third perceptual factor concerns the visual relation between question and answer. If an answer box to be ticked is provided on the printed page this needs to be near the end of the question (Wright, 1978). Printers have a tendency to align the text with the left-hand margin and the boxes with the right-hand margin irrespective of the inches of white space left in between. It would be unfortunate if this common practice were to serve as a model for CRT displays.

So far we have been considering the perceptual requirements of the form-filler, but the public are not the only 'users' of forms: forms are multipurpose documents, used by administrators as well as form-fillers. Administrators too have their perceptual requirements. Research has shown that the legibility of the answers which form-fillers provide is reduced when these answers are written so that each alphanumeric character is entered into a separate box (Barnard and Wright, 1976; et al., 1978). Perhaps such constraints are simply a temporary characteristic of hybrid data-collection systems which combine print, key punching and computer analysis. Alphanumeric information provided by the public may need completely different systems (see below), but these answers can easily be made available in any appropriate sequence or format for administrators working at visual display terminals. Indeed one of the advantages of the new technology is that the order in which the information is collected from the public does not have to be the order in which the information is displayed for administrative purposes. Both groups can have their own user-oriented sequence.

In summary it would seem that many of the perceptual factors determining the legibility of print will also apply to electronic displays and, although the latter may have some specific legibility problems, it offers significant advantages at the level of overall perceptual organization.

Comprehending

The language problems on forms can also be divided into three kinds. There are the difficulties caused by jargon and unfamiliar or specialized phrases (e.g. 'fortified wine'). There are difficulties caused by particular sentence structures which may have too many qualifications and subordinate clauses. There are difficulties caused by particular question-asking devices, for example where the question is spatially segmented with part of the question occurring in one place, such as at the head of a column, and part of the question being elsewhere, such as at the end of a row (Wright and Barnard, 1978). The direct transfer of information from print to a computer-driven display will not necessarily alleviate these problems. Nevertheless the new technologies do offer a potential for reducing the difficulties in each of these areas. The software can alert the form designer to the occurrence of jargon (Frase, 1980; Frase et al., 1980). Moreover because only one question need be dealt with at a time there is ample scope for clearly explaining the intended meaning of each question. No longer is it necessary that for reasons of saving space the explanatory notes must be relegated to the back page or some odd corner. The question, incorporating any necessary adjunct material, can be presented in full on the screen. Another way of providing assistance might be to have permanently available to the form-filler a button labelled HELP. The function of this button might be to take the user through a more detailed paraphrase of the question. There might even be a case for the system automatically opting for such a sequence if the delay in responding exceeded some criterion value, thereby reflecting the form-filler's uncertainty.

The extra space available for asking each question may make it easier to depart from the conventional style of prose text. This is one way of dealing with some of the problems of complicated sentence structures. For example, questions dealing with conjunctions and disjunctions may be easier to deal with if presented some other way, perhaps as a table or flow chart (Wright and Reid, 1973). However it is probably necessary to guard against the introduction of too much variation between questions. Before a question can be answered, form-fillers have to grasp the macro-structure of the question itself, in the sense of understanding what sort of answer they are to give, whether free response, multiple choice, yes/no or whatever. It might be expected to appear easier to the form-filler if these macro-structures are fairly similar from one question to the next.

Computer presentations may also reduce some of the problems with the more complex question-asking devices such as matrices. One way that matrix-type questions can be handled by computer is to take them essentially column by column, or row by row. In such a presentation system the screen would display two constant pieces of information, perhaps corresponding to the column heading and the response instructions (or multiple-choice answer list) and one varying piece of information corresponding to the row heading. Clearly the spatial and typographic characteristics of the presentation will be critical to the success of such a system of interrogation. There does not yet seem to have been much research in this area, but from work done on people's use of printed tables, such a move would seem likely to be helpful to form-fillers (Wright and Barnard, 1975).

In summary there seems good reason for thinking that the new technologies may help to reduce the amount of gobbledy-gook on forms although investigations of specific presentation features have not yet been undertaken.

Responding

It has been demonstrated for a range of questions that the form-filler may understand what is being asked, and may know the answer yet may provide inaccurate information on the form because of the way the answer had to be indicated (Wright, 1978). One common source of difficulty in printed forms is in complying with the instruction 'Delete the item that does not apply.' People find it much easier to respond affirmatively to what does apply than negatively to what does not (Barnard et al., 1979). Although the use of a light pen leaves the negative response available as an option in the new technologies, it is much more likely that form-fillers will be responding via a key-board or a touch panel (Bird, 1977; McEwing, 1977). Here it is conventional that people select the items that do apply. Problems only arise when these selections have to be coded into alphanumeric symbols, for example for keyboard entry. Again it has been shown that the complexity of this coding system can easily cause the wrong information to be recorded on the form (Wright, et al., 1977).

For public use in public places a minimal keypad such as the push-button telephone might suffice, with the multiple-choice options simply being numbered, or touch panels might be viable. In either case it may be appropriate to provide the form-filler with visual feedback about the choice selected before proceed-ing to the next question, and in both cases error-correction facilities have to be provided by the system. One possibility might be to provide the form-filler with a paraphrase of the answer selected and ask for a yes/no decision about it (for example after selecting the category of vehicle licence required the paraphrase question might be 'Are you applying for a licence to drive a heavy goods vehicle?'). The answer 'No' could result in the original question reappearing. The disadvantage of such a procedure is that it inevitably lengthens the time for form filling and may feel unacceptably patronizing to the form-filler.

The need to respond via a keyboard clearly imposes a number of constraints on the kinds of question that can be asked of people who are not trained typists. It would seem impracticable for example to expect name and address information from some sections of the public. One solution might be to make such information available via a magnetic strip on a plastic card, much as is done for customer identification on credit cards. The answer to a demand for 'name, address and national insurance number' would then be to insert the appropriate card into the machine. Such a card might however be seen as a step in the direction of a universal passport and might be opposed for this very reason. On the other hand it might be seen as a key for unlocking some of the mysteries of the welfare system, and as such might be found very acceptable. A great deal could depend on just how the public were introduced to such a system.

Related to the problem of error-correction on forms is the fact that when completing a printed form, form-fillers have a hard copy in front of them which can be checked and changed at will. Those relying on their forms being completed by other people obviously have different problems because different memory constraints will affect any cross-checking of information from various sections of the form. This will also be the case with auditorily presented forms. In principle, checking facilities can be provided for soft-copy visual displays, but whereas with print the form-filler is accustomed to knowing how to turn pages and scan, controlling a CRT display can mean learning some new skills for locating information, changing it, adding to it or deleting it. Moreover if the form-filler has been taken through a branching sequence by the computer software, then finding at the checking stage that a mistake was made early on could result in considerable confusion about what now needs deleting and what new questions must be answered. On a printed form the consequences of particular answers for other sections on the form may be more apparent, or form-fillers may make independent assessments about the relevance of different sections of the form regardless of the instructions given. With a fully 'user-friendly' support system the problems are not insurmountable but they do point to a class of difficulty which has no close counterpart on the majority of printed forms.

This analysis of the difficulties of forms as they relate to the perceptual, linguistic and response demands placed upon the form-filler suggests that these three classes of cognitive factors will be important no matter what the medium of presentation. It is possible that the new technologies can be used to reduce some of the problems encountered with printed forms. It is also possible that without adequate analysis of just what cognitive activities the form-filler is engaging in when answering questions, the transfer of query techniques to a new technology might make it even harder to contend with official information. Such a conclusion seems likely to apply also to the presentation of information in leaflets.

Leaflets

Although the principles relating to the design of leaflets are essentially similar to those which have been discussed for forms, nevertheless the different characteristics of the material itself mean that different design issues are involved. For example, as with forms there are perceptual factors which influence the ease of using a leaflet. However, unlike forms, which tend to be completed in a serial fashion, leaflets are frequently used by people looking for very specific information. Consequently readers use headings and other typographic cues within the text to help in this search task (Waller, 1979). Designers seeking to assist such tasks sometimes find it useful to incorporate colour to supplement other typographic variation such as change in font, weight or size. Indeed when compared with print the more limited range of typographic options available on CRT displays may increase the need for a judicious use of colour (where judicious means functional rather than decorative: see Reynolds, et al., 1978). Alternatively the nature of the reader's search task might be explicitly recognized in the design of an interactive system which could assist the reader in locating the relevant sections without the conventional page-by-page search. However this might mean prefacing the reader's encounter with the leaflet by some sort of interrogation, and it is not known what effects this might have on the reader's willingness to read the information.

Not only does the longer paragraph structure of the text in leaflets mean that the reader of an electronic leaflet will be faced with solid screenfuls of text, but many leaflets are produced in cleverly folded ways in order that the information from one part of the leaflet can be used in conjunction with information from other parts. For example the text on welfare benefits often refers to figures given in tables elsewhere in the leaflet. This cross-comparison of different pieces of information is relatively simple in a leaflet; it is a familiar practice for handling printed materials. Using soft-copy displays with similar flexibility may require training in some kind of 'command language'. It seems likely that training will be necessary however few the commands needed and however close to English the command terms manage to be. This restriction may have the effect of reducing the range of members of the general public who are willing or able to use the system. It is possible that the simultaneous use of more than one display screen may be a design option that allows the reader to continue operating in a more conventional desk-top mode for comparing and contrasting different pieces of information. A section of a screen dedicated to particular classes of information could be an alternative option (e.g. Baeker, 1979). This too may have its problems. For example it may have the dual consequences of reducing the overall amount of space available for particular categories of information and also of introducing rulings marking the boundaries of various sections of the screen. In short the risk is one of visual clutter.

One of the important constituents of many leaflets is a tabular array. The problems of designing such arrays provide a microcosm of the problems of designing leaflets. There are perceptual factors relating to both legibility and the perceptual grouping of items to assist reading across rows and between columns. There are search factors which have been shown to be systematically related to the design of the table (Wright and Fox, 1970). There are linguistic factors involved whenever the reader is making comparisons between the tabulated values and other information (Wright and Barnard, 1975). In fact the suggestion has been made that there are a great many similarities in the underlying psychological processes between reading prose and reading tables (Wright, 1980), so it seems likely that the design features which assist the users of printed tables will also apply to tabular arrays presented electronically.

Returning to leaflets, one way of exploiting the new technology is to consider the effect of *ad hoc* printing of leaflets with just the information that the user wants. The electronic storage of the information would mean that it could readily be updated, which is often a problem with printed materials. The question arises as to why a version would need to be in hard copy form at all. This perhaps relates to the responses readers make to written information. Many readers find it helpful to annotate as they read, marking sections of special relevance, noting queries and so on. Although it is possible in principle to provide such a facility with a soft-copy display it is fairly unlikely that this would be part of a public facility. Moreover since the purpose of such annotation is for future long-term reference it would scarcely be practicable to provide the storage needed at a terminal in a public place such as a post office, where many leaflets are picked up. For people accessing the information on private terminals it would be much more realistic to think of copying an annotated text for future reference. But again there are problems with the training needed by the general public if they are to be able to avail themselves of these more sophisticated options. They are probably only viable for certain sections of the community interested in certain classes of information.

A quite different way in which the new technologies may be able to improve on the present design of printed information is by making feedback of various kinds available to writers. A number of word-processing systems are now being developed which incorporate 'spies' that watch out for spelling mistakes, over-long sentences and undesirable vocabulary (see Frase, et al., 1980). The spies can provide readability formulae and point to a variety of potential trouble spots in the text. Software facilities also enable the writer to experiment in making major changes to the layout and look of the page (see Baeker, 1979). It will be interesting to see in the next few years just what meliorative effect these developments have on the ubiquitous gobbledygook of official information.

Travel information and signs

As with forms and leaflets there are perceptual factors which will determine how easily travel information can be used by the public. The legibility determinants are not necessarily the same as for reading text in leaflets or on television screens. This is partly because the information about travel is seldom sentential, being either cryptic (such as 'Diversion') or in tabular form (timetables, fare tables and so on). Another important difference is that travel information is often approached from a distance, so the reader is getting progressively more and more detailed information about the material being read. There are reasons for thinking that this changes the reading strategy for interpretation of the characters on the display (Broadbent and Broadbent, 1980).

Another important difference relating to travel information is that it is an area where auditory messages are given at present (for example station announcements) and the auditory modality may be increasingly used in the future. Drivers are already fully occupied processing visual information about the road and other road users, so it would seem to make sense to think of presenting travel information auditorily rather than visually. There are at present research projects being undertaken jointly by the BBC and the Transport and Road Research Laboratory to investigate the feasibility and acceptability of providing motorists with auditory information about critical incidents (such as road works or overturned lorries) which may have occurred in the vicinity of their route (BBC Carfax). Behavioural research has shown that simply shifting to a different sensory modality is not enough to reduce the processing load on drivers

— a great deal depends on the cognitive complexity of the message, that is to say, the simpler and less demanding an auditory message, the smaller the effect it has on concurrent visual processing (Wright, et al., 1974). If the listener has to think about the auditory information in too much detail, this will detract from the ability to attend to the visual highway. There is evidence that perceptual search problems can make very heavy demands on drivers at some roundabouts (see Smith, 1976). It is quite conveivable that the new technologies may enable travellers to preselect their destination and enter this into a search system that will then provide them with only the information that they require. Some underground stations already provide passengers with interactive facilities of this kind to supplement the standard map. Whether 'auditory maps' (especially in the form of tape cassettes) will be provided for the major trunk routes may depend on how easily and how cheaply intelligence can be provided within domestic tape recorders. It is by no means fanciful to envisage navigational aids that provide only the relevant information to travellers and do it piecemeal, thereby eliminating the difficulty of remembering what one has to do for several manoeuvres ahead. This advantage will apply to any interactive system no matter what the modality of presentation.

The typography of travel information is interesting in that it frequently encourages the reader to depart from a linear reading strategy. A typical example would be the notice which in linear order appears to advocate 'Children stop crossing'. However the typography indicates that 'STOP' is the primary message and the 'CHILDREN CROSSING' is ancillary information. When transferring messages to electronic media it is necessary to take care to preserve such distinctions. If they are lost the reader may be faced with a verbal jigsaw puzzle.

Travel information also differs from material such as leaflets in that the language makes a very heavy use of telegraphese and ellipsis. Indeed as Nickerson has pointed out, many highway messages are nonsense if taken literally, but in fact seldom pose problems for the general public's understanding of the communicative intent (Nickerson, 1979). When such problems arise the difficulties more often lie in referential interpretation of the message (for example, 'Take next turn left') rather than knowing what to do if one could actually be sure where one should be doing it.

One other common characteristic of travel information is the involvement of pictures and diagrammatic representations. It can be relatively costly, in computer storage, to digitize and display complex pictorial material. Nevertheless in some circumstances the opportunity of having a dynamic display may well make this a useful display medium. For example the highway code might become available on something akin to a video-cassette. The advantages would be that the recommended procedures for complex road manoeuvres could be illustrated using a dynamic presentation much more satisfactorily than in a static medium such as print. Commercial organizations are already providing, for topics such as heart attacks, birth control, and so on, packages that combine printed manuals, audio cassettes and computer exercises to check the reader's understanding (for example Personal Software, 1980). There would seem to be a great deal of scope for further developments in this direction for some kinds of travel information.

Given that one of the advantages of computer-based information is that it can be kept up to date relatively easily, it is perhaps surprising that little work seems to have been undertaken on digitizing map displays for the general public. New roads are opened, old roads are blocked by weather, traffic or repairs. Motorists have a real need for detailed, up-to-the-minute information about the routes they are planning to take.

In the US an experiment is being planned to link two hundred farm homes with videotelephone equipment so that farmers will have access to weather, market and agricultural information stored on remote computers ('Green Thumb', 1980). The experiment is sponsored by the US Department of Agriculture. Perhaps the UK Department of the Environment might consider whether similar schemes could be useful to road haulage companies or motorists' organizations such as the AA and RAC.

A number of design factors have been explored in relation to printed maps (see Taylor and Hopkin, 1975; Phillips and Noyes, 1977) and the technological developments in hardware make it possible now to provide the high quality of displays necessary

(Cooke, 1977) but there seem to be relatively few studies concerned with the interactive use of CRT map displays. Yet the potential would seem to be considerable. Among the more obvious facilities that might be provided by computer-controlled cartographic displays are instant scale changes (instead of the completely different maps required with printed displays); no page-turning and refolding problems; the kind of adjunct reference service (about such things as distances between places, or terrain, or demography) that only a computer-based system can supply; and, of special benefit for those of us whose first question on picking up a map is 'Where am I now?', it would be trivial to provide the display with a cursor or some other means of indicating the last known position. With the spread of in-car entertainment systems which include radio and cassette facilities, and with miniaturization of the CRT already an economic reality, the future of printed maps for motorists may be approaching an interesting crossroad, although walkers and other map users may continue to be better served by them.

In spite of the many advantages for travellers as greater use is made of interactive systems for providing travel information, it remains the case that innovative technology can sometimes be detrimental to the traveller. For example when a central installation (for example in a station terminus or departure lounge) is used to convey all the information that would otherwise be distributed round the relevant decision points, the user of the information may have legibility and memory problems which were not part of the previous system. There is nothing inevitable about the new technologies catering more satisfactorily for the traveller's needs. Everything hinges on the extent to which an analysis of those needs contributes to design decisions. It is easy to point to instances (such as the use of television displays at railway stations) where the major design determinants appear to have been the current technological limitations. This tendency must be resisted because it can sometimes generate unfortunate design precedents whereby information styles become self-perpetuating, not because they are desirable but because it is accepted that that is the way things are done. This tendency is to be seen in numerous printed displays, for example certain kinds of question occur repeatedly on forms because of the cannibalism inevitable in reaching hasty design decisions. Design is a skill and it is natural that designers should draw upon the presumed skills inherent in earlier versions. Yet this alone is not enough — knowledge about human information-processing based on the findings of psychological research has an important contribution to make to design decisions.

Speculations and conclusions

Since so much of what has been discussed in these two papers has been highly speculative it might seem both unnecessary and foolish to try squeezing the crystal ball any harder. Yet unless we consider now the potential and the problems of the electronic communication age than the technological tail will continue to wag the information-seeking dog. The cashless society in which the shopper's cheque card enables the machinery at the cash point in a store to make direct contact with the card-holder's bank account is already being envisaged. At first sight this might seem to offer much-needed advantages to those seeking welfare benefits. For example the limitations of office hours would no longer be necessary, nor would it be essential to travel to a particular local office for a personal interview if the interrogation could be done by machine and the benefit allocated directly to the claimant's bank account. Even the problem of obtaining a signature may be overcome. However there are obvious snags. By definition those eligible for welfare benefits are the economically disadvantaged. It is unlikely that the commercial banks will welcome their accounts or that their creditworthiness will be such as to gain them the vital plastic passport. Whether the national Giro banking system can circumvent this will remain to be seen, but there is clearly a risk that the new technologies will be socially devisive, widening the gap between the conventional citizen and the disadvantaged.

In other respects it is conceivable that the gaps between social strata may narrow. Information which is now the privileged domain of a few 'experts' may become more accessible to the man in the street. If you want to know the local planning laws or the time of the first train after lunch, you may no longer have to make personal contact with officialdom but can simply consult your keypad-VDU link. Whether you prefer to do this than to obtain the same information in printed form is likely to depend on factors such as how often you wish to consult the information and whether you wish to be able to use it in locations where a terminal is not conveniently available.

To recapitulate, concerning the three subfields of official information that were discussed earlier it seems probable that many printed forms will be satisfactorily replaced by electronic query techniques. The advantages to the administration come from reduced labour costs; the advantages to the public come from the speed with which the information they provide can be processed so that they can receive feed-back as to the likely outcome. Leaflets would seem destined to be with us for rather longer. Their twin advantages of portability and ease of internal cross-referencing and use in conjunction with other information sources is something that it seems unlikely that electronic media will be able to provide in the near future. Travel information is rapidly becoming electronic. Railway and bus stations are adopting electronic displays of arrival and departure information that show close affinities with the information systems developed for airports. The use of special wavebands for contacting motorists within their vehicles is technologically feasible and the economic viability is currently being assessed. Of course it is conceivable that one consequence of the eletronic communication boom will be that many people travel less. Over telephone links, word processor may talk to word processor; the need to go to the office is reduced. Yet this promise seems to have been with us for quite a long time now. Perhaps social factors will intervene: the notion that people only go to work to work will be seen for the canard that it is.

Finally, let us return to the question posed in the title of the previous paper. Will the new technologies make gobbledygook extinct? The answer appears to be a definite maybe. Certainly the potential is there. The opportunity for user-oriented design exists, and the technologies themselves offer powerful aids to the design process. Nevertheless if the potential is to be realized then it would seem essential to be able to make research findings about human information-processing available to those taking the design decisions. Such research findings have often been overlooked in the design of printed materials, where the onus may be placed fully upon readers to comprehend as best they can. The proliferation of electronic media inevitably means that the opportunities for confusion multiply. Fortunately this may necessitate a greater emphasis on the user-oriented approach to designing communications. As a consequence we may find that even official information is designed to be usable by the general public, in whatever presentation mode is appropriate.

Acknowledgements

The author would like to thank Raymond Bloomfield, Thomas Green and Richard Young for their helpful comments and advice during the preparation of this chapter. Many thanks also to Alison Emery and Julie Darling for the speed with which they transformed a labyrinth of manuscript into a readable typescript.

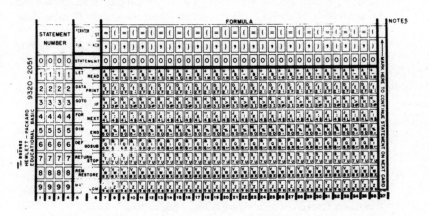

Figure 1. An IBM card designed to be read by an electronic sensing device. Human readers, when entering data onto the card, may have more problems than the machine does.

References

Adler, M. and du Feu, D.: "A computer based welfare benefits information system: the Inverclyde project." Report 0078 of the IBM United Kingdom Scientific Centre, 1975.

Atkinson, R.C.: Adaptive instructional systems: some attempts to optimize the learning process. In D. Khar (ed.), *Cognition and Instruction.* Hillsdale, N.J.: Lawrence Erlbaum Associates, 1976.

Baeker, R.: "Human-computer interactive systems: a state of the art review." Paper presented at the conference on *Processing of Visible Language,* 2, Toronto. Proceedings to be edited by P.A. Kolers, M.E. Wrolstad and H. Bouma and published by Plenum Press, New York, 1979.

Barnard, P. and Wright, P.: The effects of spaced character formats on the production and legibility of handwritten names. *Ergonomics, 19,* 81-92, 1976.

Barnard, P., Wright, P. and Wilcox, P.: The effects of spatial constraints on the legibility of handwritten alphanumeric codes. *Ergonomics, 21,* 73-78, 1978.

Barnard, P., Wright, P. and Wilcox, P.: Effects of response instructions and question style on the ease of completing forms. *Journal of Occupational Psychology, 52,* 209-226, 1979.

Bird, P.F.: "Digilux" touch sensitive panel. In *Displays for Man-Machine Systems.* Institute of Electrical Engineers Conference Publication No. 150, p. 28-29, 1977.

Broadbent, D.E. and Broadbent, M.H.P.: Priming and the passive/active model of word recognition. In R. Nickerson (ed.), *Attention and Performance VIII.* Hillsdale, N.J.: Lawrence Erlbaum Associates, 1980.

Brown, I.D., Hull, A.J. and Cox, A.C.: Digit matrices for data entry and retrieval: studies of scanning direction and colour contrast in a telephone switchboard application. *Ergonomics, 22,* 1217-1230, 1979.

Cooke, C.E.G.: High quality CRT display for command and control systems. In *Displays for Man-Machine Systems.* Institute of Electrical Engineers Conference Publication No. 150, p. 20-23, 1977.

Dickson, E.M. and Bowers, R.: *The Video Telephone: Impact of a New Era in Telecommunications.* New York: Praeger, 1973.

Frase, L.T.: Writing, text and the reader. In C. Frederiksen, M. Whiteman and J. Dominic (eds.), *Writing: the nature, development and teaching of written communications.* Hillsdale, N.J.: Lawrence Erlbaum Associates, 1980.

Frase, L.T., Keenan, S. and Dever, J.: Human performance in computer aided writing and documentation. In P.A. Kolers, M.E. Wrolstad and

H. Bouma (eds.), *Processing of Visible Language*, 2. New York: Plenum Press, 1980.

'Green Thumb': 'Green Thumb' systems. *BYTE, 5*, (2), 70, 1980.

Hultgren, G.V. and Knave, B.: Discomfort, glare and disturbances from light reflections in an office landscape with CRT display terminals. *Applied Ergonomics, 5*, 2-8, 1974.

Jones, S.: *Design of Instruction*. Training Paper 1, Department of Employment and Productivity. London: Her Majesty's Stationery Office, 1968.

McEwing, R.W.: Touch displays in industrial computer system. In *Displays for Man-Machine Systems*. Institute of Electrical Engineers Conference Publication No. 150, p. 79-81, 1977.

Nickerson, R.: "Signs". An unpublished paper available from the author at Bolt, Beranek and Newman Inc., Cambridge, Mass., 1979.

Personal Software: Personal Software 'Vitafacts' series, [trademark of Medifacts Ltd.] *BYTE, 5*(2), 51 (advertisement), 1980.

Phillips, R.J. and Noyes, L.: Searching for names in two city street maps. *Applied Ergonomics, 8*, 73-77, 1977.

Reynold, L., Spencer, H. and Glaze, G.: "The legibility and readability of viewdata displays: a survey of relevant research." Report available from authors at the Royal College of Art, 6A Cromwell Place, London SW7, 1978.

Smith, G.S.: Just how many accidents are caused by bad road signs? *Applied Ergonomics, 7*, 157-158, 1976.

Taylor, R.M. and Hopkin, V.D.: Ergonomic principles and map design. *Applied Ergonomics, 6*, 196-204, 1975.

Tinker, M.A.: *The Legibility of Print*. Ames: Iowa State University Press, 1965.

Waller, R.: Typographic access structures for educational texts. In P.A. Kolers, M.E. Wrolstad and H. Bouma (eds.), *Processing of Visible Language*, 1. New York: Plenum Press, 1979.

Wright, P.: The comprehension of tabulated information: some similarities between reading prose and reading tables. National Society for Performance and Instruction Journal, 1980, in press.

Wright, P.: "Strategy and tactics in the design of forms." Paper presented at the NATO conference on *Visual Presentation of Information* Het Vennebos, The Netherlands. Conference proceedings to be edited by R. Easterby and H. Zwaga and published by John Wiley and Sons, New York, 1978.

Wright, P. and Barnard, P.: Effects of 'more than' and 'less than' decisions on the use of numerical tables. *Journal of Applied Psychology, 60*, 606-611, 1975.

Wright, P. and Barnard, P.: Asking multiple questions about several items:

the design of matrix structures on application forms. *Applied Ergonomics, 9*, 7-14, 1978.

Wright, P. and Fox, K.: Presenting information in tables. *Applied Ergonomics, 1*, 234-242, 1970.

Wright, P., Holloway, C.M. and Aldrich, A.R.: Attending to visual or auditory information while performing other concurrent tasks.

Wright, P. and Reid, F.: Written information: some alternatives to prose for expressing the outcomes of complex contingencies. *Journal of Applied Psychology, 57*, 160-166, 1973.

Wright, P., Aldrich, A. and Wilcox, P.: Research note: some effects of coding answers for optical mark reading on the accuracy of answering multiple choice questions. *Human Factors, 19*, 83-87, 1977.

6. DESIGNING FOR THE NEW COMMUNICATIONS TECHNOLOGY: THE PRESENTATION OF COMPUTER-GENERATED INFORMATION

LINDA REYNOLDS
Graphic Information Research Unit,
Royal College of Art,
London, UK

1. Introduction

The printed word has now been with us for several hundred years. Over the centuries, craftsmen printers have gradually built up a rich fund of experience in relation to the many typographic design decisions which must be made in planning a piece of printed material. Latterly the value of many of the design principles traditionally adopted by printers has been demonstrated by objective studies of legibility. Today the presentation of conventionally typeset and printed information is generally the responsibility of a typographic designer and/or a printer, both of whom will bring specialist training and experience to bear on the problem.

Increasingly, however, computer outputs of various kinds are replacing the conventionally typeset and printed word. Where the computer is used to drive graphic-arts-quality photo-typesetting equipment, the process still falls within the realm of the printer and all but a few of his traditional design practices will still be relevant. A very different situation occurs, however, when the information is produced in the form of computer printout or Computer Output Microfilm (COM), or on a Visual Display Unit (VDU) of some kind. Although some of the basic design principles established in relation to the printed word can still be applied, some cannot. Each of these media has its own possibilities and limitations in terms of typography and layout and must be considered in its own right. As we shall see, computer displays generally impose very severe design constraints, and the successful presentation of information can therefore pose some very challenging problems.

Although a great deal of research has been carried out on the ergonomic aspects of the design of computer display equipment, relatively little attention has been paid to the typography and layout of the information on the display. Furthermore, the presentation of computer-generated information is generally outside the domain of the designer or printer and is instead the responsibility of computer personnel who will not necessarily have a sufficient level of visual awareness to tackle the problems successfully. Their primary consideration is often the convenience of the presentation from the point of view of the computer system rather than from the point of view of the user. The advice of an information designer is rarely sought because neither the producers nor the users of the information realize that the presentation could be greatly improved, often by a few simple changes which would cost little or nothing. Many people assume that computer-generated information must automatically be difficult to use and do not question its design. The designer therefore has an essential contribution to make to the effective use of the new communications technology.

2. The importance of good presentation

Presentation is important for two very good reasons. First, the overall appearance of the display is likely to affect the user's approach to the information. It may influence his feelings about whether the information is likely to be easy or difficult to use, or even whether it will be worth his while attempting to use it at all. This consideration is particularly important in cases where users may already be prejudiced against the medium, as is often the case with microforms. Both microforms and VDUs undoubtedly do have disadvantages as reading media, and it is therefore all the more important that the presentation of the information should be optimal. Visual appearance is particularly important in situations where potential users are not a captive audience, as is the case with COM library catalogues for example.

The second reason for the importance of presentation is that it affects the ease, speed and accuracy with which the information can be used. Information which is badly presented may have the advantage of using the minimum amount of space possible or requiring the minimum amount of programming effort, but this once-only saving must be weighed against the time wasted and mistakes made by perhaps hundreds or even thousands of users as a result.

3. The requirements for good presentation

With many kinds of computer-generated information, all but a few of the factors affecting legibility are outside the control of the designer. We are mainly concerned here, therefore, with the way in which the overall structure and sequence of the information is presented. In order to show the structure clearly, it is necessary to have some visual means of emphasizing, dividing and relating items of information. It will then be possible to emphasize important items, to divide items which are functionally unrelated to one another or which are different in kind, and to relate items which do have a functional relationship or which are of the same kind.

In printed materials, the necessary distinctions would normally be made using a mixture of 'typographic coding' and 'spatial coding'. By typographic coding is meant devices such as changes in type size, style or weight, and the use of additional characters such as parentheses. By spatial coding is meant the arrangement of items of information in relation to one another. This includes the use of devices such as line spacing, indentation, the use of columns and so on.

In most kinds of computer-generated output, the possibilities for typographic coding are extremely limited. For this reason it is essential that the information should be adequately coded spatially. Unfortunately, however, the possibilities for the layout of the information are also somewhat restricted.

4. Display characteristics

4.1 Character generation

Computer printouts are produced by a number of methods, including impact printing, ink jet printing and thermographic printing. Some impact printers work on the same principle as the typewriter — they carry a raised image of each individual character — but on most printout devices the characters are built up from a matrix of dots. The characters are therefore relatively crude in form and limited in number and the image quality is often poor, particularly where several copies are produced simultaneously.

Although there are in existence COM recorders which are capable of producing graphic-arts-quality output in conventional typefaces, this kind of output is too expensive for many kinds of application. The most commonly used COM recorders produce a 'utility font' by means of either a 'shaped beam cathode ray tube' character generator or a 'dot matrix' character generator. In the first case the characters are held on a disc in stencil form (see Figure 1) and are exposed onto the film by means of an electron beam. In the second case the characters are generated from a matrix of light-emitting diodes which is typically 9 dots high by 5 dots wide. The shaped beam characters are somewhat less crude in form than the dot matrix characters. Some COM recorders offer a choice of two different character sizes, but these cannot usually be mixed.

The characters displayed on VDUs are generated by several different methods. Some are vector-generated, which means that they are in effect 'drawn' on the screen, while others are generated from a dot matrix. The size of the dot matrix varies considerably, for example it may be 10 x 8, 9 x 7 or 9 x 5 dots. The vector-generated characters are generally preferable to dot matrix characters. As with COM recorders, some VDUs offer a choice of two character sizes. On the more sophisticated models it is possible to manipulate character forms and sizes at will, but such displays are used mainly for specialist purposes.

Figure 1. A typical character set for a shaped beam generator.

4.2   Implications for information design

4.2.1   Typography Although the methods of character generation differ in these three media, from a design point of view the
resulting character sets have some important features in common.
In most cases the characters are monospaced and displayed in
fixed positions, and the character set is limited to a single font
consisting of capitals, lowercase letters, numerals and certain
special characters.

The system of character spacing has possible implications for
legibility, and it also affects the appearance of the output from
an aesthetic point of view. Because each character occupies the
same amount of space regardless of its width, narrow letters
such as *i* and *l* tend to become isolated. This creates an uneven
texture which most typographers would find aesthetically dis-
pleasing. It is not known, however, whether the additional cost
of producing proportionally spaced displays would be justified
in terms of improvements in legibility. A further implication of
this inflexible system of spacing is that adjacent words can only
be separated by whole numbers of blank character spaces —
usually one. The fixed character and word spacing sometimes
result in strong vertical rivers of space running through the text,
which can be distracting. They also make right-hand justification difficult or impossible to achieve, though its value is in any
case questionable as far as legibility is concerned.

The limited character set means that there is very little scope
for the typographic 'coding' of information. Some printout
devices, COM recorders and VDUs can produce bold and even
italicized characters, but their visual impact is generally not as
great as that of conventionally printed bold and italic characters. In most cases, therefore, the only way of typographically
coding information is to use capitals or additional characters
such as parentheses or asterisks. While capitals may be acceptable in certain circumstances for coding main headings or
emphasizing important words in text, their use should be kept
to a minimum. Research has shown that words in capitals are
less easily recognized than words in lowercase because they lack
the distinctive outline created by the ascenders and descenders
of lowercase letters (Spencer, 1969). Furthermore, blocks of

text in capitals will tend to have a very solid and daunting appearance, whereas the variation in the height of lowercase letters creates more space between lines and gives the text a more open and accessible appearance. Underlining should also be avoided wherever possible, because interlinear spacing is often minimal and the underlining may fuse with the letters above and below. It is also likely to interfere with the perception of the word shapes, and for this reason it should not be used with capitals. If underlining cannot be avoided (in headings for example), it should be followed by a line of space. Double underlining should never be used, as it is extremely ugly.

Some VDUs and most teletext and viewdata receivers have a colour facility. It is then possible to colour-code items of information. Great care is needed in the use of colour in this way, however, because the colours will vary in their luminance, and hence in their legibility and their apparent 'dominance' when viewed on the screen. It is therefore important to use only the most legible colours and to use them in a logical way — just as typographic variations might be used — to convey the structure of the information (Reynolds, 1979a).

4.2.2   Layout The possibilities for information layout in many kinds of computer-generated display are considerably restricted by unsuitable line lengths and inflexible line spacing.

A typical line length for computer printouts is 132 characters. Lines on COM may be up to 138 or 160 characters long depending on the character size, and on many VDUs the length is 80 characters. However, where television receivers are used as VDUs (as in teletext, viewdata and small personal computer systems) the line length is usually only 40 characters. The optimum line length for conventionally printed materials has been shown to be between 50 and 60 characters and spaces (Spencer, 1969), and there is no reason to suppose that the optimum for computer-generated information will differ very greatly from this. Very much shorter lines will interrupt the natural pattern of eye movements too frequently, and very much longer lines will make it difficult for the eyes to make an accurate return sweep from the end of one line to the beginning of the next. In order to save space and to keep the cost of materials to a minimum there is a tendency for line lengths to be used to the full, though lines of only 80 characters are often used on printouts.

On most printouts and VDUs, line spacing is totally inflexible. On COM it can often be set at a desired value at the beginning of a production run, but once set it cannot easily be varied. For the sake of economy, most forms of computer output have relatively close line spacing. This is detrimental to legibility for several reasons. In extreme cases the letters on adjacent lines may fuse, and this will be especially noticeable with output which is in capitals only. If the line spacing is less than the word spacing, then each word will be closer to those above and below it than it is to those which precede and follow it. The words will cease to hold together as lines and the lines will therefore be more difficult to follow. Close line spacing will also exaggerate the effect of excessively long lines, making it even more difficult for the eyes to make accurate return sweeps. The only way of increasing line spacing on many displays is to leave alternate lines blank, but this usually results in excessive spacing and is very uneconomical. It can also be counterproductive because the information becomes fragmented over a much larger number of frames. This is a particularly important consideration with VDUs, some of which can accommodate only 32 or even 24 lines per frame, as opposed to the 60 or so lines available in most other forms of computer output.

5. The design of continuous text

In designing continuous text for display on printouts, COM or VDUs, it is very important to choose a suitable line length. This should ideally not be more than 60 characters and certainly not more than 70. With printouts and COM offering line lengths of over 130 characters, the most economical solution may be to divide the page or frame into two columns of 50-60 characters each. It is not worthwhile attempting to justify the right-hand margin of the text, because this will result in a high percentage of lines ending with a hyphenation, and in irregular word spacing. Both of these are likely to impair legibility, as well as being ugly in appearance.

Wherever possible, text should be displayed in uppercase and lowercase characters. As a general rule it should be 'set solid', that is with characters on every line, but where the line spacing can be set at will it is better to err on the generous side. Successive paragraphs should be separated by a line of space. This will break up the text and give it a more inviting and accessible appearance. On a page or frame carrying 60 or so lines, the text should be broken into at least three or four paragraphs, and ideally it should be written with this requirement in mind.

In most cases, headings will be required within the text. A numbered system of headings will help readers to appreciate the structure of the text at a glance, but ideally no more than three levels of heading should be used. The section numbers should be displayed in the margin if possible. Headings should preferably be in lowercase lettering, though it may be necessary to use underlining. Main headings in underlined lowercase lettering might be drawn out into the left-hand margin. Subheadings might then be in underlined lowercase against the left-hand margin, and subheadings in a similar position but without the underlining. Alternatively capitals might be used for main headings, or bold might be used if it is available. The typographic coding of headings should always be supported by a logical system of spacing. Main headings should be preceded by more space than subheadings, and each heading should be closer to the text which follows it than it is to the end of the preceding paragraph.

The greatest problem in presenting text with headings arise in relation to displays with only 24 lines of 40 characters each. Here space cannot be used too generously to compensate for the lack of typographic coding or the information will become too fragmented. In this situation facilities for colour-coding headings can be extremely valuable.

With all computer-generated text — and indeed other kinds of information too — it is always worth considering whether it is in fact necessary to divide the information into 'pages'. Unless each page or frame is itself divided into two columns, there is often no reason why the information should not run on in a continuous scroll-like sequence.

6. The design of structured text

A good example of 'structured text' is the library catalogue. The typical catalogue consists of a series of entries arranged in some logical order, each entry in turn consisting of a number of different elements. In this kind of material, it is necessary to distinguish between the different elements within each entry while ensuring that each entry still appears as a coherent whole, and to emphasize that element of each entry which determines its place in the alphabetical or numerical sequence. In some cases other elements may need to be emphasized too.

An example of a relatively successful presentation (on COM) is shown in Figure 2 (Reynolds, 1979b). Here the entries are arranged in alphabetical order by either author or title. Author entries and title entries are readily distinguishable from one another by the capitals used for authors' surnames and by the fact that authors' names stand alone on a line. Searching through the listing for a particular author or title is made easier by the indentation of the body of each entry, the simplicity of this system of indentation enhancing its effectiveness. Essential information needed for finding or ordering the book is separated from the body of the entry by a line of space so that it stands out clearly, but the entries still hold together as units because of the generous spacing between them. The fact that all of the information is ranged left also helps to hold each entry together. If some items of information are ranged right, this tends to fragment the entries, and it is often not clear to which entry such items belong.

In the example shown in Figure 2, each frame has been divided into two columns in order to create an acceptable line length. To some extent, however, it is a disadvantage to break an alphabetical sequence within each frame. A continuous vertical sequence would be preferable, but this would be extremely wasteful of space using the line length shown and given the present standard frame size.

WALLING, Desmond Eric
Fluvial processes in instrumented watersheds: studies of
small watersheds in the British Isles; edited for the British
Geomorphological Research Group by K.J. Gregory and D.E.
Walling. London, Institute of British Geographers, 1974.
iii,196p. (Institute of British Geographers. Special
publications. no.6)
... papers ... read at a meeting of the British
Geomorphological Research Group held in Exeter from 11 to 13
... 1972 ... Conclusion
Key: English text. French and German abstracts
Bibl. Control number:0901989169

Shelved at : M 1.3 GRE
Book number: 073184

WALLON, Armand
Histoire de la France rurale, sous la direction de Georges
Duby et Arma ... allot. (Paris), Seuil, c1975-. v. (Collection
L'Univers h ...ique)
Includes bib ... ographies and indexes
t. 1. Ber ... G. et al. La formation des campagnes
françaises. -- 2. Neveux, H., Jacquart, J. et Leroy Ladurie,
E. L'âge r... sique des paysans. Control number:lc75519433

Shelved at ... 18.1044 HIS
Note 19 ... have Tome: La fin de la France paysanne de
... 05 ... par Michel Gervais, Marcel Jollivet
et ... Tavernier, 1976.

WALRAFF, Gunter
Der Aufmacher: der Mann, der bei Bild Hans Esser war (von)
Gunter Wallraff. Koln (i.e. Cologne), Kiepenheuer & Witsch,
1977. 240p. Control number:3462007316

Shelved at : D 2.6 WAL
Book number: 076359

The walls of Acre: intergroup relations and urban development.
New York, Holt, Rinehart and Winston, (1974). xvii, 140 p.
(Case studies in cultural anthropology)
Bibliography: p. 139-140. Control number:lc74008726

Shelved at : D 9.5694 RUB
Book number: 076168

WALMSLEY, Keith
Butterworths company law handbook; edited by Keith Walmsley.
London, Butterworth, 1978. 1362,25p
Index. Control number:0406143102

Shelved at : JRM 6 BUT
Book number: 078208

WALPOLE, Robert, Earl of Orford, b.1676
... and Bert ... with ... the relation of politics to literature,
... and Bertram A. Goldgar. Lincoln, University of
Nebraska Press, (1976).
Includes bibliographical references and index. Control
number:lc76000609

Shelved at : MA 448.P66
Book number: 075994

Walpole and the wits: the relation of politics to literature,
1722-1742, Bertrand A. Goldgar. Lincoln, University of
Nebraska Press, (1976).
Includes bibliographical references and index. Control
number:lc76000609

Shelved at : MA 448.P66
Book number: 075994

Walt Whitman, The correspondence: supplement, edited by Edwin
Haviland Miller. New York, New York University Press, 1977
Includes an index as well as corrections and additions to
vols. 1-5 of The correspondence. Control number:lc76025786

Shelved at : MB 3200.F61
Book number: 066612

WALTER, Eugene Victor
Terror and resistance: a study of political violence with
case studies of some primitive African communities, by Eugene
Victor Walter. New York London, Oxford U.P., 1969. xiii,385p.
(Terror and society)
bibl p367-374. Control number:0198311750?

Shelved at : H 4.2060 WAL
Book number: 005810

WALTER, Henriette
La phonologie du (francais), (par) Henriette Walter. (Paris),
Presses universitaires de France, 1977. 16cp. (Le linguiste;
18). Control number:st3001283?

Shelved at : M3C 102 WAL
Book number: 077780

Walter i que es tuliste ?(por) Ana Maria Moix. Barcelona,
Barral, 1973. 259p. (Hispanica nova; 55). Control
number:8421102359

Shelved at : MM 6663.0345
Book number: 042960

7. The design of lists, indexes and tables

The essential feature which lists, indexes and tables have in common is that they usually consist of two or more columns of data. Having selected an item from one column, the user generally needs to follow that item horizontally across the page to extract further information about it from other columns. In this kind of situation it is very important that the columns should not be so far apart that there is a risk of error in reading across. Very wide column spacing such as that shown in Figure 3 is common in computer-generated information however. Sometimes this is because the columns are deliberately spaced out to fill the available line length for the sake of creating a 'balanced' display, or because the column headings are too lengthy. In other situations wide spacing is unavoidable, perhaps because the information in some columns varies considerably in length, or perhaps because information is missing from a particular column for several consecutive entries. The problem can sometimes be overcome by rearranging the order of the columns, or in extreme situations by truncating a small number of very long items, but it will not always be possible to bring the column spacing within desirable limits by these means. It is then necessary to give the user some positive help in reading across from column to column. An experiment on a COM display consisting of single-line entries in a two-column list suggested that the most effective and pleasing devices were the use of a line of space or a horizontal rule after every fifth entry (Reynolds and Spencer, 1979). Leader dots were equally effective but less pleasing in appearance. Double line spacing (using alternate lines only) was helpful with very wide column spacings, but under normal circumstances it was a disadvantage because the index then occupied twice as many frames and took longer to search. Heavy vertical rules should be avoided in tabular materials, as they will tend to draw the eye down the page instead of across it.

With very complex tables the line length of the display may not be great enough to accommodate all of the columns required. This situation often results in displays such as that illustrated in Figure 4. This layout is extremely unsatisfactory. It is difficult to scan down any one column because of interference from

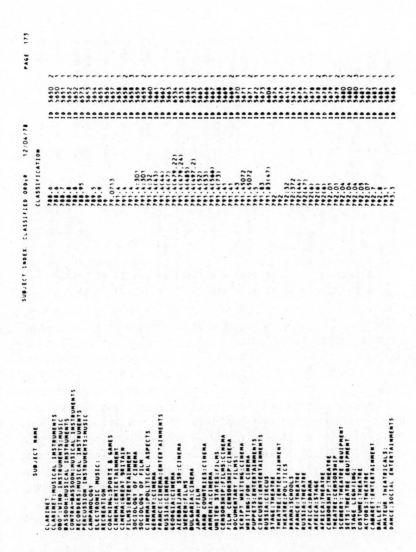

Figure 3. An example of excessively wide column spacing.

```
                                                                          SUPPLEMENT                                          PAGE   44
          AUTHOR              TITLE &          PAGINATION &   PUBLISHER &         PLACE OF       YEAR  PRICE EDITION     ISBN
                               CLASS            COLLATION       LOCATIONS         PUBLICATION           £
BALCHIN, NIGEL
          FATAL FASCINATION - A CHOICE OF CRIME               HUTCHINSON          LONDON         1964  1.05              S0000003431 0
                    364.152                       200P        04  MS/02 SU/04 WM/71
          IN THE ABSENCE OF MRS PETERSEN                      COLLINS                            1966  1.05              S0700015023 5
                    F                                         16  BH/53 BH/15 DA/09 FX/07 MD/14 MD/13 MY/11 NT/16 SF/01 SL/54 SL/51
                                                              SU/12
          THE ANATOMY OF VILLAINY                             COLLINS             LONDON         1950  0.63              S0700109504
                    301.151                       256P I      02  MS/02
          A WAY THROUGH THE WOOD                              COLLINS                            1970  1.25              0 00 221937 9
                    F                                         01  DA/01 WM/71
BALDER, ALTON PARKER
          THE COMPLETE MANUAL OF SKIN DIVING                  COLLIER-MACMILLAN   LONDON         1968                    S0700053823 0
                    797.23                        302P BIK    04  AL/04
BALDICK, ROBERT
          THE SIEGE OF PARIS                                  BATSFORD            LONDON         1964  1.75              S0700152418 0
                    944.08                        248P BIK    00  OS/66
BALDWIN, FRANK ARNOLD
          SIMPLE SHORT WAVE RECEIVERS                         DATA PUBLICATIONS   LONDON         1970  0.80              0 900328 06 1
                    621.384151                    140P ID     07  CM/01 MS/07 MS/06 WM/02
BALDWIN, JAMES
          THE FIRE NEXT TIME                                  JOSEPH              LONDON         1963  0.67              S0700017057 0
                    323.173                       112P        06  MS/05 OA/06 WK/01
          TELL ME HOW LONG THE TRAIN'S BEEN GONE              JOSEPH                             1968  1.75              S0700031417 0
                    F                                         08  BR/07 DO/08 MD/05 MS/06 MD/04 OA/01 OS/66 SL/51 ST/52
          NOBODY KNOWS MY NAME                                JOSEPH              LONDON         1964  1.05              S0700062477 0
                    323.173                       196P        02  DO/02
          THE FIRE NEXT TIME                                  WATTS               NEW YORK       1963  2.20     NEW.  0 531 00312 4
                    323.173L                      120P        03  BR/01 MD/03 MS/02
          THE DEVIL FINDS WORK                                CORGI               LONDON         1978  0.75     NEW.  0 552 10663 1
                    791.430909352                 125P        01  MD/01
          GO TELL IT ON THE MOUNTAIN                          JOSEPH                             1954  2.50              0 7181 0161 8
                    F                                         03  BH/52 BH/51 BH/62 MS/03 SR/02 WR/01
          GIOVANNI'S ROOM                                     JOSEPH                             1957  2.00              0 7181 0475 7
                                                              19  BR/13 BY/03 FX/15 ML/17 MS/18 MY/14 MY/02 MY/71 NT/19 WM/16
BALDWIN, MICHAEL
          THE GREAT CHAM                                      SECKER & WARBURG                   1967  1.38              0 436 03202 3
                    F                                         08  BR/08 HL/07 SP/04 SR/06
   ...M, NICK
          FARM TRACTORS                                       WARNE               LONDON         1977  3.95              0 7232 2060 3
                    629.225                       64P IK      12  BY/11 HL/05 MY/01 LU/10 OS.04 OS/06 OS/09 SL/03 SL/12 SU/08 WM/04
                                                              WM/07 WK/02
BALFOUR, ALEXANDER
          BASIC NUMERICAL ANALYSIS WITH FORTRAN               HEINEMANN           LONDON         1977  2.90     2ND.  0 435 77484 0
                    519.4 FORTRAN                 287P BIK    02  SL/02 WM/01
BA..FOUR, MICHAEL
          THE KAISER AND HIS TIMES                            CRESSET P           LONDON         1964  2.50              S0700020519 0
                    943.084                       524P BIT    02  NT/02
      BRIAN NEVILLE
          DEATH OF A LOW HANDICAP MAN                         BARKER                             1974  1.96              0 213 16465 5
                    F                                         06  AL/04 MD/03 ML/06 LU/01 OS/05 SF/02
          TIMEPIECE                                           DOBSON                             1968  0.90              0 234 77223 9
                    F                                         07  MD/07 SR/06 ST/51 WM/71
BALL, FRANCES
    *     THE DEVELOPMENT OF READING SKILLS                   BLACKWELL           OXFORD         1977  3.50              0 631 18290 X
                    372.4                         120P I      04  MQ/04 NT/02 OS/01 SL/03
BALL, JOHN
          COPS AND ROBBERS                                    DEUTSCH             LONDON         1978  4.95              0 233 96887 3
                    364.162                       200P IK     01  SL/01
PRINTED ON 14 JUL 1978                                                                                                      BAL - BAL
```

Figure 4. The confusing effect of overlapping columns and insufficient spatial separation of entries.

other data, and it is difficult to tell which items belong to which entry because there is insufficient space between entries. With displays of this kind it is often worthwhile to consider whether it is in fact necessary from the user's point of view for the data to be presented in so many different columns. In many cases the layout merely reflects the structure of the computer file. If the same data were presented in fewer columns, the layout could be greatly simplified and the information would be easier to use.

A more satisfactory approach to this kind of problem is shown in Figure 5, where turnover lines have been created within columns. With this quantity of information in each column, however, the multi-column layout may not necessarily be the best approach. The layout shown in Figure 2 will be easier to use from the point of view of finding an item of information within a particular entry, though the multi-column layout is likely to promote faster alphabetical searching through the file because it presents the user with an unbroken sequence of entries. However the double column layout does have the additional advantages of being more flexible in terms of the amount of information it can accommodate, and for longer entries it uses less space.

The problems of presenting tabular information satisfactorily are particularly severe in the case of displays having only 24 lines of 40 characters each. In this situation it is often necessary to restructure the information in order to present it in a comprehensible and easily usable form.

8. Conclusions

The successful design of computer-generated displays requires new ways of thinking on the part of both designers and computer personnel. The designer must come to terms with the limitations and the potential of each of the various output media. The systems analyst and computer programmer must begin to think in terms of the needs of the ultimate user of the information, rather than designing outputs which are simple to produce. In this context it is important to remember that users

Dewey	Author	Title	Accession
338.272	NEF ,JOHN U	THE RISE OF THE BRITISH COAL INDUSTRY VOL. 1	T10885692 J
338.272	NEF ,JOHN U	THE RISE OF THE BRITISH COAL INDUSTRY VOL. 2 66	T10885706 J
338.272	PLATT ,JOHN	BRITISH COAL : A REVIEW OF THE INDUSTRY, ITS ORGANISATION AND MANAGEMENT 68	T10585834 X
338.272	POLITICAL AND ECONOMIC PLANNING	REPORT ON THE BRITISH COAL INDUSTRY : A SURVEY OF THE CURRENT PROBLEMS OF THE BRITISH COAL-MINING INDUSTRY..., FEBRUARY 1936 [36]	T10588019 X
338.272	ROBENS ,ALFRED ,BARON ROBENS	TEN YEAR STINT 72	30493874Z B C D F H J K L M N O P S T U Y
338.272	ROBINSON ,COLIN ,B.1932	THE ENERGY 'CRISIS' AND BRITISH COAL : THE ECONOMICS OF THE FULL MARKET IN THE 1970S AND BEYOND 74	255360576 R
338.272	SIMPSON ,E S	COAL AND THE POWER INDUSTRIES IN POSTWAR BRITAIN 66	T10675337 C
338.272	SMITH ,RAYMOND	SEA-COAL FOR LONDON : HISTORY OF THE COAL FACTORS IN THE LONDON MARKET 61	T10707972 X
338.272	TREATY ESTABLISHING THE EUROPEAN COAL AND STEEL COMMUNITY, PARIS, 18 APRIL 1951 73 (CMND 5189)		101518900 R
338.272	TREATY ESTABLISHING THE EUROPEAN COAL AND STEEL COMMUNITY, PARIS, 18 APRIL 1951 [NEW ED.] 72		115901132 R
338.272 / 338.2728	WHITE ,C J	AN INTRODUCTION TO THE COAL MINING INDUSTRY 71	854750363 C O
338.2728	DEPARTMENT OF ENERGY	DEVELOPMENT OF THE OIL AND GAS RESOURCES OF THE UNITED KINGDOM HMSO 75	114102384 R
338.2728	DEPARTMENT OF ENERGY	DEVELOPMENT OF THE OIL AND GAS RESOURCES OF THE UNITED KINGDOM...; A REPORT TO PARLIAMENT... APRIL 1976 76	114102767 R
338.2728	DEPARTMENT OF ENERGY	DEVELOPMENT OF THE OIL AND GAS RESOURCES OF THE UNITED KINGDOM : A REPORT TO PARLIAMENT... PARIL 1977 HMSO 77	114102988 R
338.2728	DEPARTMENT OF ENERGY	PRODUCTION AND RESERVES OF OIL AND GAS IN THE UNITED KINGDOM HMSO 74	115111298 R
338.2728	DEPARTMENT OF ENERGY	UNITED KINGDOM OFFSHORE OIL AND GAS POLICY 74 (CMND 5696)	101569602 R
338.2728	ORGANISATION FOR ECONOMIC CO-OPERATION AND DEVELOPMENT	THE EXPLORATION FOR AND EXPLOITATION OF CRUDE OIL AND NATURAL GAS IN THE OECD EUROPEAN AREA INCLUDING THE CONTINENTAL SHELF : MINING AND FISCAL LEGISLATION 73	T10997962 R X
338.2728	ABELS ,JULES	ROCKEFELLER MILLIONS - THE STORY OF THE WORLD'S MOST STUPENDOUS FORTUNE 67	T10001549 C D G H M O
338.27282	ABIR ,MORDECHAI	OIL, POWER AND POLITICS : CONFLICT IN ARABIA, THE RED SEA AND THE GULF 74	714629901 D
338.27282	ANDERSON ,J R L	EAST OF SUEZ : A STUDY OF BRITAIN'S GREATEST TRADING ENTERPRISE -BRITISH PETROLEUM CO 69	340109750 C J
338.27282	BRITISH NATIONAL OIL CORPORATION	REPORT AND ACCOUNTS 1976 77	906049008 R
338.27282	CAIRNCROSS ,FRANCES	THE SECOND GREAT CRASH : HOW THE OIL CRISIS COULD DESTROY THE WORLD'S ECONOMY BY FRANCES CAIRNCROSS & HAMISH MCRAE METHUEN 75	413334406 D E
338.27282	CHEVALIER ,JEAN-MARIE	THE NEW OIL STAKES ALLEN LANE 75	713909072 C E
338.27282	COMMISSION OF THE EUROPEAN COMMUNITIES	THE COMMUNITY OIL SECTOR MEDIUM-TERM FORECAST AND GUIDELINES [74]	119359919 R
338.27282	COOPER ,BRYAN	ALASKA - THE LAST FRONTIER 72	091109701 C D

Figure 5. The use of turnover lines within columns (a line of space between entries would have improved this layout however).

of computer-generated information now include a wide spectrum of people, many of whom know nothing about computers or computing. This means that not only must the information be set out clearly, but it must also be as free as possible from unnecessary abbreviations and computer jargon. The use of abbreviations may save fractions of a second in response time and it may reduce data storage costs, but this must be weighed against the risk of users puzzling for several minutes over the meaning of the display, possibly making mistakes in using it, and possibly becoming discouraged or irritated.

However, although the presentation of most computer-generated information – whether on paper, microfilm or VDUs – leaves a great deal to be desired, there are signs that a small number of information producers and users are beginning to question the quality of the output. Where users are able to choose between alternative information sources, or indeed to choose whether or not they use the information at all, the information producer who consciously attempts to provide a high standard of visual presentation within the limitations of the medium is likely to hold a commercial advantage over his competitors. It is to be hoped, therefore, that the growing awareness of the importance of information design will have a snowball effect and that we shall see an improvement in the presentation of computer-generated information. There is a limit to what can be done within the potentialities of the existing hardware however, and what is ultimately needed is for equipment manufacturers to provide more sophisticated character forms, a greater range of typographic variation and greater flexibility of layout. This, though, is unlikely to come about until the purchasers and users of the equipment demand a better quality of output and are prepared to pay for it.

References

Reynolds L
'Teletext and viewdata: a new challenge for the designer'. *Information Design Journal 1* (1), 2-14, 1979a.

Reynolds L.: 'Visual presentation of information in COM library catalogues: a survey'. British Library R & D Report 5472, 1979b.

Reynolds L and Spencer H.: 'Two experiments on the layout of information on Computer Output Microfilm'. London: Graphic Information Research Unit, Royal College of Art, 1979.

Spencer H.: *The Visible Word*. London: Lund Humphries, 1969.

7. ELECTRONIC ALTERNATIVES TO PAPER-BASED PUBLISHING IN SCIENCE AND TECHNOLOGY

DONALD W. KING
King Research, Inc.,
Rockville, Maryland, USA

This paper is based on two studies performed for the National Science Foundation in the United States (1,2). These two studies served to expose four basic publishing myths. One myth is that journals are contributing to an information explosion. To the contrary, the number of journals has been expanding steadily in the United States over the last few years, but from 1960 to 1979 the number of scholarly scientific and technical journals has only increased from 2,800 to 4,600 (there were double that number in each year if trade journals, bulletins and so on are considered). There are about 400,000 articles published in the 4,600 journals, and this number increases about 2 to 4 per cent per year. The growth in number of journal articles published is highly correlated to the number of scientists and engineers in the country, a number which has been increasing by about 2 to 3 per cent per year over the past two decades.

The second myth is that journals are never read. Journals are read. In fact on average they are read a great deal. In a recent survey we observed that journal articles are read about 600 times a year on the average which means that there are about 50,000 readings for average journals. Some articles have many more readings and a high proportion of them have very few readings. This phenomenon is represented by a very highly skewed distribution of reading of the articles.

Another myth is that journal publishers are queuing up waiting to file for bankruptcy. There is just too much evidence to

This paper was presented at the Association of American Publishers' symposium on "New Formats for Publishing: Alternative Media and Auxiliary Techniques", New York, 24 September 1979.

the contrary — studies by Professor Fritz Machlup and Kenneth Leeson (3) at New York University and Princeton, the Capital Systems Group study (4), the University of Indiana study (5) and some studies that we have done (6,7) suggest that most journal publishers are doing very well. Although some are having difficulty, the majority certainly are not. Not only is their gross revenue healthy but their cash flow is very favourable.

The fourth myth is that all current journals will become electronic journals in the next decade. This also is just likely to happen. I do think that electronic processes will become prevalent with all the journal system participants, including authors, publishers, libraries and readers. However it is likely that all but a small proportion of the journals will continue to publish in a paper form or a combination of a paper form and an electronic form.

From a technical and systems standpoint, scientific and technical journals have not changed a great deal in the past three hundred years. The published journal is still similar to the original scholarly journals published in the 1600s. In the United States, the journal publishing industry has grown steadily over the past two decades and is expected to do so in the future. However, a number of current events could dramatically alter the journal system as we now know it. First, there is a revolution taking place concerning the quantity of articles that are distributed in separate copies as opposed to being distributed in bound journal issues. Of the number of readings of 250 million readings that take place, there are about 30 million readings from articles distributed through this channel. This is nearly as many readings as take place through library subscriptions. The distribution channel, in separate copies, includes both interlibrary loans and individual separates such as reprints distributed by authors and publishers. Secondly, advances in library networking and resource sharing may soon reach the point where there will be a formal national periodical system in this country. Finally, advancements in electronic processing will almost certainly yield enormous advantages to future scientific and technical information transfer. Many of these advances are taking place outside the scientific and technical information transfer in such areas as office word processing, telecommunications, technology in non-scientific publication, online biblio-graphic searching, minicomputers, mass digital storage and others.

Advances in technology which will have a significant effect on authorship are electronic word-processing and text-editing systems. Later I will discuss how this technology will have a second-order effect on other system functions as well. Electronic word-processing and text-editing systems have already achieved widespread use. Word-processing systems involve editing-type-writers that use magnetic digital storage of one form or another. There are also text-editing systems that range from terminals that tie into a local computer to intelligent terminals with self-contained memory and microprocessor-based computer func-tions. These systems help achieve improvements in editorial quality of manuscripts and they provide faster and more reli-able input. However their most direct advantage comes from substantial reduction in secretarial labour costs. Other advan-ced technologies that may assist authorship are teleconferencing and online bibliographic systems. Online computer systems are being used more and more frequently as a medium of interper-sonal communication among groups of individuals who are separated by time or space. This form of communication can upgrade authorship by facilitating much more extensive informal feedback which in turn supports the preparation of a manu-script before submission to a publisher. The increase in prepar-ing manuscripts in digital form would complement or enhance teleconferencing. Also online bibliographic searches will prob-ably improve the quality of background research and thus the quality of articles. The advance in electronic technology will not only improve the quality of articles and increase the speed of preparation but will also reduce costs somewhat in the future.

Electronic processes are also currently being used extensively by publishers for editing, reduction and composition. Direct in-put from authors to publishers in digital form would reduce the cost of keyboarding even more. Optical character recognition (OCR) might also be used increasingly for direct input. However the technology and costs of OCR have improved much more slowly than many have anticipated in the past. Rita Lerner (8) has pointed out that one obstacle to total computer photocomposition of scientific and technical material has been the problem of setting complex mathematics or display equations. However, several software packages have been developed to deal with this, such as a system which was developed for the American Institute of Physics based on software developed for the US Government Printing Office and the Bell Laboratories Unex system. These software packages are capable of setting different mathematics using an almost unlimited set of special characters. It is not yet possible to integrate a mathematic page make-up programme with illustrations but in the future one can expect to have full-text computer photocomposition including illustrations, charts and figures. Computer photocomposition that can handle complex mathematics is priced competitively with typewriter composition and can be purchased on the open market.

In the future, publishers will have an enormous flexibility in the form and mode of distribution of articles made from master images. Electronic technology has progressed to the point where articles can be individually printed directly from computer output. Impact printers cause problems with this kind of output but non-impact printing has resolved the problem of computer output speed. The ink jet, electrophotographic and electrostatic systems all hold substantial promise for scientific and technical publishing in the future. Computer master images can also be transformed into microform or onto videodiscs. Microform still has many disadvantages but Joyce Russel (9) mentioned some other uses of microform that I think make a great deal of sense. The new videodisc technology also holds a great deal of promise for distribution and storage but also has some weaknesses since video-images cannot display adequate full-printed page on most inexpensive viewing devices. Charles Goldstein also discusses videodisc technology (10).

Another area in which electronic processes might be employed is in mailing digital tapes, cards or discs of manuscripts prepared by word processing so that publishers could enter the text directly into a composer. Also the digital text could be transmitted to publishers by telecommunication. Reviewers could also be included in a teleconference-like remote access system.

Electronic processes will also affect librarians in the future.

I think that we all recognize that the average number of library subscriptions is expected to drop in the future. Even though there is not direct evidence, it would appear that libraries may be substituting interlibrary loans for purchases of journal subscriptions. Certainly the number of interlibrary loans is high, around 5.3 million in the US in 1977, and is increasing. One of the manifestations of increased interlibrary loans is a plan for a new system for enhancing future interlibrary loan needs, the national periodical system. This is discussed by Sue Frankee (11).

If the Copyright Clearance Center (CCC) is successful, it could serve as a central facility for distributing copies of articles. Even though the CCC has gained some acceptance from publishers, it has encountered a lack of acceptance from many libraries. If this barrier can be overcome, its handling of photocopying, transaction and accounting for royalty payments could make the CCC a candidate for a central facility such as a national periodical center. Also, organizations such as the Center for Research Libraries, the Institute for Scientific Information and the University Microfilms International are all handling requests for copies of journal articles and could expand their operations to serve as a central facility.

The extreme interest shown by both the public and private sectors in distributing copies of articles suggests that the time may be near for some form of a national periodicals system in the United States.

One of the areas in which new technology has been directly applicable to scientific and technical information transfer is in library operations and services. The most prominent of these are computer-based bibliographic searches, automated circulation, cataloguing of books and interlibrary loan processing. One development outside scientific and technical communication that might make a great impact is that of mass storage memories. If a national periodicals system comes into being, one component might be a digital storage of input directly from publishers. Thus far, the most likely is magnetic tape segmented for mechanical handling, however some output problems associated with queuing delays are making the cost prohibitively high at the moment. Other barriers to mass electronic storage are the needs for costly labour-intensive

104 *Donald W. King*

indexing and control and more effective access software. Abstracting and indexing services play an important role in providing the intellectual analysis and organization of scientific and technical literature and thus allowing effective access to articles by scientists and engineers engaged in research activities. Toni Carbo Bearman discusses this issue (12).

Another information product is the bibliographic database. These are increasingly becoming an information product in their own right. Covering in general the same literature as do the traditional products, they allow in-depth searching of large volumes of information stored by the computer. As development of bibliographic databases has increased, related service organizations include processors and suppliers who make the data available and brokers who perform computer searches for users.

Technology will probably have less immediate impact on journal readers than on other participants because their function lends itself less to such development. However in the long run it is likely that users will begin to receive copies of article text by electronic communication through digital output and videodisplays.

Transmission is an important function and is discussed separately because of its potential effect on the future journal systems. Currently journal transmission primarily involves mailing or personally transferring manuscripts of articles. This function is characterized by a large number of individual transmissions which do not cost a great deal in relation to other costs, but are very slow. In fact, rapid transmission in one form or another may be the most important electronic process involved in the future. At this time, very little, if any, transmission of the full text of articles is performed electronically. Exceptions are the one existing electronic journal in computer technology and · occasional articles sent by telefacsimile. In addition, some messages about articles, such as online bibliographic data, library cataloguing, and requests for interlibrary loans are sent by telecommunication. Most telecommunication is by voice-grade telephone lines. Moreover, value-added networks provide a potentially low-cost telecommunication capability for all participants in scientific and technical communication.

These recent technological advances, which were developed largely independently of scientific and technical information transfer, provide all the components of a comprehensive electronic journal system. Such a system would provide an enormous flexibility. The principal strength of this flexibility is that individual articles can be distributed in a manner most economically advantageous to them. I might point out that US publishers distribute 2.5 billion articles manually to libraries and individual subscribers. That is an impressive number! Our estimate of the total amount of reading each year is about 250 million, so there are about ten article copies distributed by publishers for every one that is read, which means that there is some inefficiency in the system. There is a great deal of reading and a great deal of reading of individual articles, but there are a lot of them being sent out and not many of them being frequently read. The frequently-read articles may still be distributed in paper form while infrequently-read articles can be requested and quickly received by telecommunication when they are needed. The trade-off is that resources currently wasted in printing, mailing and storage would be applied to better identification and retrieval of information thus reducing cost, improving quality and increasing efficiency. Other benefits of electronic processing can also be derived. We believe better systems integration will yield more emphasis on the quality of article content, less republication of articles for updating purposes or for different audiences, and better access to and retrieval of information needed in multidisciplinary research.

In a comprehensive electronic journal system, articles will be prepared by authors using sophisticated text-editing systems; article preparation may include joint writing of text through teleconferencing systems in which immediate peer review is possible, comments are made and specific research questions can be answered. Furthermore, many of the citations used in the article will come from those found in online bibliographic searches. When citations are identified, they can be immediately retrieved by telecommunication in full-text on CRT or paper form.

The digital form of the unreviewed manuscript will be directly transmitted electronically to the publisher. The publisher, in turn, will electronically transmit the manuscript to a subject editor who will read the text by CRT or printout and make electronic notes concerning editorial and content quality. The subject editor may choose appropriate reviewers using a computer program that matches the profile or potential reviewers with topics covered in the article. Other computer-stored information will also be used to help screen reviewers, such as by affiliation and relationship to the authors, status of the most recent review, frequency of reviews, timeliness of response of previous reviews, and quality of reviews. The reviewers will respond to editors and the editors, in turn, to authors by telecommunication comparable to current tele-conferencing processes. Publishers and editors can also use electronic processes for business purposes, address listings and other activities. An accepted article would then be subject to redaction on a text-editing terminal and computer-based text would be output in several forms including full-text and bibliographic description. The bibliographic description will be transmitted electronically and used directly by search services or will be entered into abstracting and indexing services for further analysis and processing.

The full text will be sent electronically to some individual scientists designated by the author, or by request to scientists based on their topic, author, or other bibliographic identifier. The scientists may receive the text on personal terminals or on their library terminals. Articles would also be sent directly by telecommunication to a national periodicals system should this come about. Telecommunicated requests for copies of articles will be satisfied with full text telecommunicated to the requesters.

The electronic processes also provide a great deal of flexibility of output which can enhance reading and assimilation of the information. End users could request alternative formats of the text that would suit their particular needs for example for rapid scanning or for in-depth reading. Rapid scanning can be facilitated by highlighting certain elements of the text, narrowing column widths, widening spaces between lines and through other techniques. Human-factors modifications can likewise help in in-depth reading. Electronic processes can also aid in combining mathematical formulae, data presentations, and text in a way that meets alternative needs.

This comprehensive electronic journal is highly desirable and currently achieveable. It is believed that within the next twenty years a majority of articles will be handled by at least some electronic processes throughout the system, but that not all articles will be incorporated into a comprehensive electronic journal system like that just described. Some articles will be processed electronically in different ways depending on the electronic capabilities of the senders and receivers involved.

There are some major constraints involved in adoption and use of a comprehensive electronic journal. One of the principal constraints to any electronic information transfer system is the lack of incentive of the system participants to change. For example, authors publish partially for the prestige and recognition which results in professional advancement. Certainly the 'publish or perish' environment that exists in some fields of science and in some organizations creates an incentive to publish. Therefore, any alternative communication system must meet this perceived need. Many publishers lack a financial incentive for drastically deviating from the current journal-publishing practices. While many book and small journal publishers appear to have financial problems, most large publishers are doing very well financially: they earn a comfortable margin on income and they require much less capital to publish journals than books since the income from subscriptions is received before most costs are incurred. Return on investment for journal publishing is therefore very favourable. Substitution of royalty payments for subscription income will lessen this advantage since photocopying takes place over a long time-period. The current value of royalty income is less than the value of an equal amount of subscription income. Thus any new publishing systems must incorporate some financial incentives as publishers are unlikely to want to change. Another problem is that some income is derived by publishers through sale of advertising, which appears to be precluded by distribution of separates. However, it has been suggested that advertising can be focussed on specific scientists with advertising interest profiles and can itself be distributed as a separate. This system may be much better than current advertising practices (13).

Scientists as users also present some barriers to new systems that directly impact upon their behaviour (14). It has been claimed for many years that scientists would quickly adapt to the direct use of computer terminals and would search bibliographic databases online. However, while some scientists do this, most still rely on an intermediary to perform their searches for them. This occurs in part because many scientists have no easy access to terminals and in part because some are reluctant to use them (15). Regardless of the reasons, if an alternative journal-publishing and distribution system involves direct online communication some incentives to use it must be provided to scientists, and their behaviour must be altered. We believe that, in the future, new scientists who have been trained on terminals in high schools and universities will find it unacceptable not to have these facilities available for analysis, text processing, search, retrieval, and other forms of communication.

Libraries, while they have been in the forefront of adopting online searching as an information tool, often have little incentive to change their mode of operating unless their patrons and funders desire such a change. While many libraries currently are automating for cataloguing and internal record-keeping, they still require motivation to change their procedures in dealing with scientists. So again, some outside incentive will probably be necessary.

Other constraints are technological. Standards must be set for word-processing and text-editing output so that publishers can receive it and easily convert it to the appropriate format. A major problem exists in treating non-textual input, including tables, mathematical formulae and graphics such as line graphs, photographs, and chemical structure diagrams. Technologically, graphics can be electronically handled now, but the economics are not practical for the high volume of graphics found in physical sciences, engineering and life sciences articles. Another requirement is that the cost of telecommunication must continue its downward trend. Sending and receiving equipment must be sufficiently sophisticated to permit rapid, and therefore low-cost, communication. Mass storage devices now available could economically store nearly all current literature, but the cost of input and output will remain unacceptable until some breakthroughs in this area are made.

So while the opportunities for electronic journal processing, transmission, and access are substantial, the questions to be answered are also great. For example, are electronic communication processes better suited for popular entertainment and communication, or for economic transactions such as those envisaged for electronic funds transfer systems? Or is scientific information transfer such a complex economic and sociological phenomenon that progress will be hindered by tradition, as in any other social system involving complex interactions among numerous participants? Despite these caveats, we are very optimistic.

References

1. King, D.W., D.D. McDonald, and N.K. Roderer. *The Journal in Scientific Communication: The Roles of Authors, Publishers, Libraries, and Readers in a Vital System.* National Science Foundation Contract No. NSF-C-DSI-75-06942. Rockville, Maryland: King Research Inc., May 1979. (PB-269 263; also scheduled for publication by Dowden, Hutchinson & Ross, Inc.).
2. King, D.W. and N.K. Roderer. *Systems Analysis of Scientific and Technical Communication in the United States: The Electronic Alternative to Communication Through Paper-Based Journals.* National Science Foundation Contract No. NSF-C-DS176-15515. Rockville, Maryland: King Research, Inc., 1978.
   Annex I: Communication Functions in Science and Technology.
   Annex II: The Current Practices.
   Annex III: An Electronic Alternative.
   Annex IV: The Cost Model.
   (NTIS: PB-281 847 to PB-281 851)
3. Machlup, Fritz and Kenneth W. Leeson. *Information Through the Printed Word: The Dissemination of Scholarly, Scientific and Intellectual Knowledge.* Volume 1: *Book Publishing.* Volume II: *Journals.* Volume III: *Libraries.* New York: Praeger, 1978.
4. Huybrechts, Brigitte D. and John M. Strawhorn. *A Survey of*

110   *Donald W. King*

Publishing Policies and Practices in the U.S. National Science Foundation Contract No. HSF/IST-74/24410/13. Rockville, Maryland: Capital Systems Group, Inc., October 1978.

5.   Fry, B.M. and H.S. White. *Economics and Interaction of the Publisher-Library Relationships in the Production and Use of Scholarly and Research Journals.* National Science Foundation Grant No. GN-41308. Bloomington: Indiana University Graduate Library School, 1975.

6.   King. D.W., D.D. McDonald, and C.H. Olsen. *A Survey of Readers, Subscribers, and Authors of the Journal of National Cancer Institute.* Final Report, National Cancer Institute Contract No. N01-CO-75226. Rockville, Maryland: King Research, Inc., 1978.

7.   King, D.W., *The Journal in Scientific Communication.*

8.   Lerner, Rita. "Electronic Publishing". Paper presented at the 39th Annual Congress of the FID, Edinburgh, September 1978.

9.   Russell, Joyce. "Microforms, Pros and Cons". Paper presented at the Association of American Publishers' Symposium on "New Formats for Publishing: Alternative Media and Auxiliary Techniques"; New York, September 24, 1979.

10.   Goldstein, Charles. "Video Discs as an Alternative". Paper presented at the Association on American Publishers' Symposium on "New Formats for Publishing: Alternative Media and Auxiliary Techniques", New York, 24 September, 1979.

11.   Frankee, Sue. "A National Periodicals Center". Paper presented at the Association of American Publishers' Symposium on "New Formats for Publishing: Alternative Media and Auxiliary Techniques", New York, 24 September, 1979.

12.   Bearman, Toni Carbo. "Value of Abstracting and Indexing Services". Paper presented at the Association of American Publishers' Symposium on "New Formats for Publishing: Alternative Media and Auxiliary Techniques", New York, 24 September, 1979.

13.   Whitby, Oliver W. "Computer Architecture for External Editorial Processing". *Journal of Research Computer Studies* (to be published).

14.   King, Donald W. and Vernon E. Palmour. "User Behaviour". In: *Changing Patterns in Information Retrieval.* Edited by Carol Fenichel. Philadelphia: American Society for Information Science, 1974.

15.   Katter, Robert V. and Davis B. McCarn. "AIM-TWX: An Experimental On-Line Bibliographic Retrieval System". In: *Interactive Bibliographic Search: The User/Computer Interface.* Edited by Donald E. Walker. Montvale, N.J.: AFIPS Press, 1971.

8. EURONET DIANE – A PRECURSOR TO ELECTRONIC PUBLISHING?

FRANCO MASTRODDI
Consultant, Commission of the
European Communities,
Luxembourg

SERGE LUSTAC
Administrator, Commission of the
European Communities,
Luxembourg

Foreword

The *New York Times* publishes its articles through a computer network (the NYT Information Bank), and journals such as *Le Monde*, *Le Point*, the *Financial Times* and *Frankfurter Allegemeine* have taken or are considering similar steps. Is this the start of true "electronic publishing" and the decline of the printed word? This paper looks at current European advances by describing the online information network Euronet DIANE which opened on 13 Feburary 1980.

Introduction

Euronet DIANE is an online network for scientific, technical and socioeconomic information, and comprises:

—— Euronet: a data transmission network covering Europe and constructed by the nine postal and telecommunications (PTT) administrations of the European Community;
—— DIANE (Direct Information Access Network for Europe): an association of computerized information and documentation centres (hosts) linked to Euronet.

The aim of this facility sponsored by the Commission of the European Communities (CEC) is to open access to bibliographic

111

and factual information resources stocked in the memories of European documentation centres by rendering the computers accessible 'online' to any user in the Common Market under equitable technical and economic conditions. This article will cover the relationship between Euronet DIANE and conventional publishing, the reasons for building the network, how it works, and future perspectives.

Firstly, however, it would be useful to cover briefly the background of the network.

Background

Euronet DIANE originated on 24 June 1971 when the European Council of Ministers passed a resolution (1) to promote the development of a European information and documentation network and to favour appropriate coordination between member states' national policies. At the same time the 'Committee for Information and Documentation of Science and Technology' (CIDST) was created — comprising delegates from each Community country — to aid the Commission in its tasks.

A first plan of action (2) set out an overall budgetary programme for 1975-1977:

— development of sectoral information systems in areas of Community interest (agriculture, environment, biomedicine);
— construction of a special data transmission network (Euronet);
— promotion of new norms and standards, rational development of new techniques and methodologies.

A second three-year programme (3) was adopted by the Council of Ministers to cover 1978-1980:

— conversion of Euronet to a public operational network;
— development of a market for scientific and technical information within the European Community;
— promotion of technology and methodologists with emphasis on improving Euronet DIANE services.

Furthermore, this Council decision gave the Commission a brief to negotiate the extension of Euronet to the countries of CEPT (Conference of European Postal and Telecommunications Administrations).

Users of Euronet DIANE comprise information specialists (documentalists, librarians), engineers and researchers in almost every discipline (medicine, chemistry, law, business, economics and so on). The aim of the network is to put an efficient online tool at their disposal which will make their job of information-gathering easier and more effective.

Euronet DIANE and publishing

Any reference to the recent 'information explosion' worldwide will be greeted with either a sigh of despair or a shrug of in-difference, depending on whether one has to scan literature regularly or not.

It is estimated that 70,000-100,000 learned journals (primary publications) are published worldwide each year (4), and, in order to keep abreast of this evolution, libraries, professional associations and commercial enterprises publish regularly catalogues and indexes, abstract journals, trade directories, statistics and so on. These so-called 'secondary publications' are the concern of Euronet DIANE, for, during the photo-composition stage of printing, a computer by-product on magnetic tape which parallels the eventual paper version is created. The tapes thus collected are slightly modified and added to previous collections on a large computer, forming enormous files known as bibliographic databases (see Figure 1).

These databases can of course be searched in the same way as any library archives. A tele-typewriter (or a screen) is connected over the normal telephone line or a network to the computer which 'hosts' them, and the searcher enters appropriate commands online in the form of key-words, subject area, author's name, title of the publication, or many other flagged parts of the documents stored, such as language or year of publication.

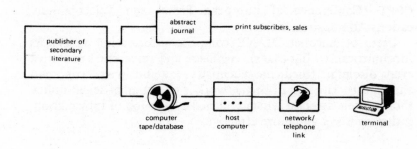

Why Euronet DIANE?

It is not necessary to emphasize the importance of technology transfer for innovation and social and economic progress, and the role of the effective dissemination of scientific and technical information in this context. The computer has become indispensable in managing the vast volumes of published information, and online hosts have been a recognized part of the US publishing scene since the early 1970s. However Europe lags behind both in production and usage of databases, to the point where European information searchers regularly use transatlantic networks to access the two or three large US hosts. (5).

Demand from Europe to the US is limited by the geographical distance, which leads to high telecommunications costs and to a lack of face-to-face contact with the host's management, aside from the interactive dialogue from user terminal to host computer.

Paradoxically, the demand *within* Europe is frustrated by other reasons:

— lack of appropriate telecommunications facilities,
— fragmentation and multiplicity of European hosts,
— absence of equipment standards,
— language barriers.

The need to overcome these obstacles led naturally to the definition of the concept Euronet DIANE:

— firstly a data transmission network of 'super telephone lines' which can provide, compared with normal international lines, reliable, quick, efficient and low-cost links to different European host computers:
— then a voluntary association of hosts (DIANE) which have agreed to offer their services without discrimination to any Community country, to adapt to the demands of an international market for their debases, and adapt theit computers to Euronet technical requirements;
— finally the continuous development of common support actions and the gradual development of tools which will facilitate usage of the network and improve its quality.

A new information tool

The first step was therefore the creation of a data transmission network, and, to this end, the CEC concluded a contract with the PTT administrations of the nine European Community member countries in December 1975. In fact the contract (and subsequent addenda) forms the legal basis for a co-funding programme to build Euronet.

Euronet. Euronet is basically a set of improved telephone lines joined by special computerized switching centres, and is particularly suited to international online information retrieval on account of its technology, configuration and tariff structure.

Technology. Euronet employs the new data transmission technology known as packet switching, employed by present and future US and European national networks. Essentially the user at the terminal end transmits a message to the host service over Euronet. The message is automatically disassembled at a switching centre, each part being flagged and interleaved with other messages during its transit, and reassembled at the other end.

This method ensures optimal usage of lines, extra error-checking facilities, and the parallel transmission of the many short messages typical of online information retrieval. The technology incorporates many internationally recognized norms which will facilitate future expansion and network interconnections (6).

Finally the technology makes Euronet an 'intelligent' network which accepts a wide variety of computers and terminals (Figure 2).

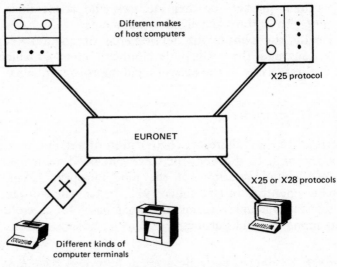

Figure 2

Network configuration. Network access points are located in each country of the European Community. A user would therefore telephone Euronet's nearest entry point over his national telephone service or possibly a national data transmission network linked to Euronet, switch through the acoustic signal (high-pitched tone) to his terminal, and then key into the terminal the codes necessary to establish a link with hosts anywhere on the network (Figure 3). Otherwise the user could directly dial the host service abroad, but international telephone lines are notoriously unreliable for data transmission, as well as highly expensive.

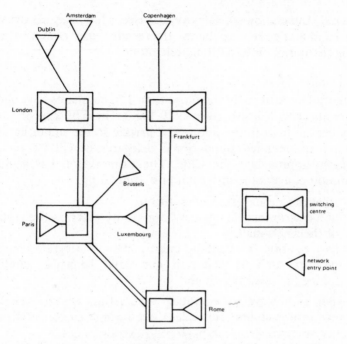

Figure 3.

Tariffs. The CEC has negotiated with the PTTs a special tariff for this totally new service. The charges are two-part; for national access to a Euronet entry point and for the international Euronet element.

The international element is *common*, that is, a call from London to Rome is the same as a call from Rome to London, and *independent* of *distance* – calls from London to any different part of the network do not vary in price. The cost of a call depends mainly on duration of connection and volume of data transmitted, thus the tariff scheme is ideal for brief, low-volume online searches.

The cost of the call from a user's telephone to Euronet depends on each country, and tends to be either the normal charge (UK, Denmark, the Netherlands, Italy) or distance-independent (Belgium, Federal Republic of Germany, France,

Ireland, Luxembourg). The overall price is low, varying between a 30 and 80 per cent saving for the terminal user compared with usng the normal international telephone.

DIANE

Twenty-five hosts offering more than 150 databases have agreed to connect to Euronet over 1979-1980. These host information services are in both the public and private sector and either have been recommended by national delegates of CIDST or have directly approached the CEC. The Commission has signed a common convention with each host stipulating:

— rules of fair and free competition;
— non-discrimination against Community users on the grounds of their nationality;
— participation in efforts to coordinate and integrate common services such as common command language, common billing facilities and so on.

DIANE is however a voluntary association where each host retains responsibility for sales, marketing, customer liaison, quality and extent of databases, and extra services.

On the whole the databases cover the 'precise' sciences and technology rather than social sciences. However present trends include a growth in demand for socioeconomic, legal and commercial databases. Some hosts are already reacting to this demand.

Support actions

The Commission is well aware of many new problems created by Euronet DIANE, and has undertaken both long-term and short-term measures. In the short term:

— a Euronet user forum has been created;
— an online enquiry service has been set up on Euronet;
— Euronet DIANE focal points have been formed in some countries, as well as a multinational trouble-shooting 'launch team' in Luxembourg;
— intermediary/referral services have been promoted for non-specialist users;
— publicity and promotion have been undertaken.

In the longer term:

— a common command language is being implemented on a number of hosts (7);
— computer translation facilities are being developed for use by hosts;
— recommendations are put forward to hosts on the co-ordination of contracts (conditions of sale), password issuing, billing and so on.

It is hoped that both kinds of measures will help reduce the socio-psychological barriers of conversing with a computer and its foreign management and of committing to memory a range of esoteric access procedures.

It should be recognized that hosts, users (whether specialists or not), PTT administrations and the Commission are undergoing a rapid, sometimes painful, learning process in the embryonic European market.

Future perspectives

Online networks and information retrieval facilities represent a powerful tool for sorting quickly and precisely bibliographic references to primary publications. Therefore the growth of services like Euronet DIANE can only stimulate the dissemination of the printed word. This could increase sales for publishers, provided they do not suffer from the common practice whereby documentation centres (libraries normally) photocopy the relevant article from their journal copy to send to the user. International legislation does not suffice to prevent this practice at present.

Another opportunity open is for the publisher to enter directly into the online information market as a database supplier. A new kind of database is increasingly in demand, containing not bibliographical references but factual, numeric or textual 'full' data or primary information. Publishers could ideally offer whole series of full articles, reports and so on online either on a sophisticated information retrieval facility as with DIANE hosts, or through the fast-growing, simpler, videotex systems. This tendency might lead to a readjustment in the aim of some publications, and to a true on-demand publishing trend where, possibly, articles are not printed unless interest is shown in the online computer version.

In the longer term, much depends on the integration of new technologies in present publishing methods. A European symposium in November 1979 (8) on this topic discussed various perspectives such as:

— publishing through videotex systems;
— improved methods for inputting masses of data to a computer (optical character reading, laser scanning);
— improved storage media (optical digital discs, storing up to 125 million characters per square centimetre);
— widespread availability of cheap, easy-to-operate terminals (noting the current French experiment to provide a terminal replacing the telephone directory);
— marriage between text processors, computer networks, and the publisher's computer.

However until more is known about the impact of these techniques on job structures, on the economics of publishing, and on consumers (it is currently difficult to browse through a computer file, or to transport a computer terminal), progress towards the 'paperless society', as far as the published word is concerned, is likely to be subject to considerable constraints.

Glossary

Online: a process where a computer terminal is used to obtain and refine responses immediately from a (remote) computer. The computer requires extra equipment to become available online over a telephone line.

Database: a computer file. Can contain millions of bibliographic references, chemical/physical properties, statistics (usually in time series), and so on.

Host (service, computer): an independent service bureau which 'hosts' or holds databases, and markets them to users.

Command language: a set of programmes which allows the user to search the databases. Characterized by strict syntax, and simple commands such as FIND A, COMBINE A AND B, DISPLAY C.

Data: here, electronic signals ('bits') storable on a computer. Are modified for transmission over telephone lines.

Intermediary: an information specialist who performs a search (online or not) on behalf of the original requestor.

Referral: provision of advice or guidance to a user, for example on which database can answer your question.

Videotex: an online information system uniting an adapted television set with a remote computer over the telephone line, generally for access to current affairs, business, financial, sports and leisure information.

References

1. Council Resolution of 24 June 1971, *Official Journal* of the EC (*O.J.*) No. C122/7.
2. 1st Action Plan. COM (74) 1423 Final.
3. 2nd Action Plan. *O.J.* L311 of 4 November 1978.
4. G. Anderla. *Information in 1985, a Forecasting Study.* OECD, Paris, 1973, pp. 14-16.
5. J.L. Hall, *Online Information Retrieval Source Book.* Aslib, London, 1977.
6. International Consultative Committee for Telegraphy and Telephony (CCITT). Recommendations X3, X25, X28, X29, X75. CCITT, Palais des Nations, Geneva.
7. A Negus. *Euronet Guidelines: Standard Commands for Retrieval Systems.* INSPEC, London, 1977.
8. "The Impact of New Technologies on Publishing", 6 November 1979. Symposium organized by the CEC, Luxembourg. *Euronet DIANE News* 17, December 1979.

9. PRESENT AND FUTURE PRINTING TECHNIQUES

YURI GATES
PIRA, Leatherhead, UK

Excluding, of course, speech, the printed word is the oldest of the mass communication media. Until this century, with the arrival of radio, cinema and television, there was no other challenger. However, in spite of earlier gloomy forebodings, the printed word has survived.

The printing industry is going through a period of rapid technological change. Factors having a dominant influence have originated outside the printing industry itself; they include computers, micro-processors, lasers, digitization of information, screen-based technology including television, and telecommunications. The significant technology changes within the next ten years or so will have their origins in one or more of these areas, rather than in the development of existing printing technology.

Data Capture: Text

The first process undertaken by the printer is to capture the author's words so that he can manipulate them. There are several ways of doing this.

Keyboarding
Keyboards are, and are likely to remain, the principal means of capturing text for typesetting. There are several types, including:

Qwerty, the standard typewriter layout, to which the majority of keyboards conform. The Qwerty keyboard is not ergonomically designed — in fact the keys are arranged

123

so as to slow the typist down (originally so that she could not work quickly enough to jam the type bars). The Qwerty keyboard is firmly entrenched and will be exceedingly difficult to displace, despite its inefficiency.

Linotype 90, a special keyboard used in some newspaper work. This design, like the Qwerty, is also less than ideal from the ergonomic point of view.

Maltron, an ergonomically designed keyboard, specially shaped to accommodate the fingers. The most frequently used characters are grouped so that they are closest to the fingers, thus enabling the data capture process to be speeded up considerably.

Chord-type keyboards, such as the Panaltype and Microwriter, which require two or more keys to be depressed simultaneously to generate a character. These keyboards are not used directly for typesetting applications, but might be used by an author for subsequent input to a word processor, which in turn might be linked to a typesetting system.

With the increasing use of word-processing machines in offices, it is likely that the author or publisher will take over more and more from the printer the initial capturing of text for subsequent printing, thus avoiding the costs of re-keying.

Optical character recognition
Optical character recognition (OCR) is a well-established technology which has been extensively used, particularly in the US, to input editorial text and classified advertisements in newspaper work. Typewritten text, in a typeface recognized by the machine, can be rapidly scanned and transformed into machine-readable form. The disadvantage lies in the difficulty of detecting hardware errors and of correcting input errors. Its use in newspapers is declining, but it is likely to continue in use in certain specialist areas, for example in directory publishing, where it is a cost-effective method of capturing large quantities of data. A further specialist application is the use of multi-font OCR, for example for republishing out-of-print works. Multi-font machines are expensive so are likely to be made accessible through bureau services rather than purchase.

Recently lower-cost OCR scanners designed for use with word-processing machines have been put on the market. They may prove to be useful data capture devices for typesetting purposes.

Voice input

Several companies throughout the world are working on the development of speech recognition systems, though not specifically for typesetting applications. Speech recognition systems are of three main types:

> Isolated speech recognizer: the utterance to be recognized, which may be a word or phrase, must be clearly delimited by initial and final periods of silence. Such devices are currently available and are suitable for control and command applications.
>
> Connected word recognizer: this allows the use of free-flowing speech to input a group of words, but the user is constrained to use only words within the predefined vocabulary, and the group must be clearly delimited by initial and final periods of silence. Devices of this type are becoming available for up to five connected words.
>
> Continuous speech recognizer: this accepts natural, free-flowing speech, with no constraint forced on the speaker by the recognition system. Devices exist but are not yet commercially available.

The speech recognition system must be trained to recognize the speakers who use it; performance is best with a single speaker. A typical current system will recognise 50-100 words with a 2 per cent error rate. The largest systems recognize about 1,000 words.

Rapidly-decreasing costs of computer storage will assist the development of voice input systems and a voice-controlled typewriter with a vocabulary of about 5,000 words may emerge within ten years. When they are fully developed and sufficiently accurate, voice recognition systems will offer considerable advantages for data input.

Hot metal

Hot metal systems produce the well-known raised type from

which newspapers and books have been traditionally printed. They are now becoming obsolete. Their main use is for updating work previously set in hot metal.

Photosetters

Photosetters are machines which produce images on photographic film or paper in the layout and design required for the printed page.

The original (first-generation) photosetters replicate the hot metal process. The second-generation machines, including direct-entry machines, hold negative-film masters of characters on a disc or drum and use optical systems to vary the type size. The third-generation machines use digitally stored characters which can be electronically enlarged, reduced, slanted and emboldened. A large number of typefaces and print sizes can be created. Digitization also provides the potential of producing pictures as well as text, and machines which can output both text and pictures are already becoming available. This trend will continue. Fourth-generation machines (only one of which is commercially available) use lasers for imaging. Resolution is 1,000 dots/inch and output speeds of about 1,000 lines/minute can be achieved. Better and cheaper laser systems will be developed. Fourth-generation machines, like third-generation machines, have the advantages associated with digitization — the capability of being linked with computer systems and the potential for producing pictures as well as text.

Direct-entry photosetters
Direct-entry photosetters are comparatively inexpensive to buy and are getting cheaper as the microprocessors they contain get cheaper. They are simple to operate. They can have counting keyboards (both horizontal and vertical counting) which enable hyphenation to be undertaken or setting of mathematics to be done. Their major disadvantage is the difficulty and expense of correcting a major error.

The latest devices incorporate visual display units and floppy disc systems; some are programmable to cater for different modes of operation such as inputting, editing and correcting.

An important development is the interfacing of word processors with direct-entry photosetters. Potentially this enables a typist to produce graphic-arts-quality work.

Offline photosetting systems
Offline photosetting systems consist typically of a number of independent keyboards producing paper-tape or floppy-disc input for an editing/correcting visual display unit which may or may not be capable of justification and hyphenation. Sometimes a line printer is attached to the VDU as a proofing device. The output from the VDU is a paper tape or floppy disc which goes into the typesetting unit. Compared to the direct-entry photosetter, these systems have greater speed and versatility (more typefaces, more special characters, vertical justification and so on), but they are being superseded by online systems.

Online photosetting systems
Both batch and interactive online systems are available. They consist of centralized computing facilities to which (1) data capture devices, including visual display units, OCR devices, paper-tape equipment, wire services and so on, and (2) typesetters and line printers, can be linked. The command structure for the system is independent of the typesetter, which enables much more complex work to be undertaken. Rigid discs are used to store programs and data. With the interactive systems justification and hyphenation are done continuously, and quite complex page make-up can be done automatically.

Full-page composition

Full-page composition systems enable text to be arranged into completed pages automatically by electronic data processing.

Electronic full-page composition is now available for book work. Parameters which specify the page layout, including depth, width, where to place pictures and tables and so on are entered as well as rules for vertical justification. Page numbers and running heads for verso and recto pages can be inserted automatically, as well as footnotes.

Three systems are available for full-page composition of newspaper and magazine pages. The individual pieces of text which are to make up a page are brought together, given instructions related to the position and area they are to occupy, and then displayed on a screen. If the result is incorrect, the pieces can be adjusted or moved. Spaces of the required size can be left for illustrations. One system is capable of displaying the picture in position too; it also offers the option of outputting text and pictures on microfilm. These systems are expensive and they have not become widely accepted yet, but they are symptomatic of a new approach to the handling of text and pictures for reproduction.

Graphic reproduction

Although the main discussion is of the printed word, it is worth a small diversion to consider the printing of illustrations. Graphic reproduction is the process by which the printer converts an original photograph or artist's original into a set of dots which, when printed, will reproduce the tones of the original. This has traditionally been done photographically by means of a half-tone screen, but recent years have seen the introduction of scanners using lasers capable of converting continuous-tone pictures into digital form. An electronic screen is used to break the picture down into dots; no physical screen is involved. Software is used to convert dot density into half-tone values. In simple systems the output from the scanner is dumped onto a magnetic disc which can then be input to a photosetter, thus enabling pictures to be integrated with text. In more sophisticated systems this is done online.

At present very fine screening is not possible, because there is a trade-off between quality, which is a function of the number of bits of information data capable of being assigned to each dot, and speed of operation (the more bits of information data, the longer it takes to process them). The current practicable upper limit of screening is about 40 lines/centimetre, but the limit will be lifted upwards as costs of computer memory and access fall.

Systems integrating text and pictures are likely to develop rapidly. They offer the potential for increased production speeds and reduced labour costs.

Copy-to-plate systems
The idea of outputting text and pictures directly onto film via a photosetter can be extended still further to outputting directly onto a printing plate. Such systems are currently being developed, including one based on KC film.

Colour scanning
Analog-type colour scanners have been available for a number of years for making colour separations and are still being developed and improved. Their principal limitation is the necessity for converting analog colour data into digital form for subsequent page make-up. Digital-type colour scanners which are of more recent introduction do not have this limitation. They have greater software capability which enables more complex colour-modelling functions to be used, thus permitting more exact colour rendering to be obtained. Digital scanners and their associated page make-up systems are costly and are likely to be installed only in the larger printing firms and trade houses. Their advantage is to reduce the amount of labour-intensive montage or assembly work required, thus reducing costs.

At the other end of the scale are marketed small and comparatively inexpensive analog scanners which are suitable for the smaller printer who wishes to produce colour separations in house.

Printing processes

Lithography
Lithography is a versatile process used in many types of printing, including book work and magazine printing. It has developed rapidly over the last two decades until it is now the dominant printing process. This has been due both to its ability to take

advantage of developments in computed-aided typesetting and electronic composition, as well as to its ability to satisfy a market need for reasonably priced colour work.

Sheet-fed machines are usually used for short-to-medium-run work while web-fed machines are used for longer runs, but there is a trend away from the larger sheet-fed machines toward narrow web machines in the larger sizes. The use of these narrow web machines (less than eight-page A4 size) is increasing because they can more easily be used with in-line equipment, such as in-line sheeters and folders. Although the publisher must accept some limitation on page sizes with narrow web machines, he is likely to get better value since the printer can build up a more efficient production system with in-line equipment.

Gravure
Gravure has two main fields of application: publication work and packaging. It has the ability to print at high speed and give a good result even on relatively low-quality paper. It can produce high quality illustrations in black-and-white or colour, which leads to its use in long-run magazine and colour-supplement work. The major technological problem to be overcome is the high cost of preparing gravure cylinders; if this is solved, gravure could challenge the dominant position of lithography. There are signs that a new system of cylinder making, using laser engraving, may be commercially available in two to three years time, in which case gravure could be viable for print runs down to 250,000 copies. Cylinder preparation seems ideally suitable for EDP application which would lead to simplification of the process, higher speeds and reduced cost.

Letterpress
Letterpress, the original printing process, is in a state of decline. Research has shown that pressure distribution in letterpress printing is a fundamental limit preventing it attaining the quality achievable with lithography or gravure. No new letterpress machines are being designed and current technological development is directed at extending the life of existing equipment. Newspapers, formerly printed exclusively by letterpress,

are changing over to web offset. Metal plates are becoming obsolete but polymer plates will continue to be used on reel-fed rotary letterpress machines for the production of paperback books where high-quality half-tone work is not required.

Non-impact printing processes

Ink jet printing

Ink jet printing is based on Rayleigh's discovery that a jet of liquid issuing from an orifice will break into droplets if it is vibrated at a certain frequency. These droplets are extremely uniform in size and are very evenly spaced.

A charged electrode is placed near the point at which the droplets break from the jet so that each drop will have on it a charge directly proportional to that on the charged electrode. The droplet stream then passes into an electrostatic field, normally maintained by two deflector plates, and the charged droplets are deflected in a direction perpendicular both to the jet axis and to the substrate passing beyond the deflector plate. The distance the droplets are deflected is proportional to their charge, which is in turn proportional to the voltage applied to the charged electrode whilst the drop was forming from the jet. By suitable choice of the parameters governing drop charging and deflection, a drop of ink may be placed anywhere within a narrow band on the substrate passing beneath the jet. Droplets unwanted for printing may be deflected to an ink catcher or gutter; the ink collected in the gutter is then pumped away and recirculated.

Ink jet printing utilizes the output from digitally-stored, computer-processed information, from which the parameters to place each drop of ink in the correct positions on the substrate are derived. Unlike the traditional printing processes, where every copy is identical, ink jet printing allows each copy to be different, if so desired. Applications include mailshot letters and personally addressed magazines and newspapers; there are several others, from carpet printing to cheque coding. Potential applications include colour facsimile, colour printout from viewdata terminals, and on-demand publishing.

Some ink jet printers utilize a single jet, some have an array of jets, though most have less than ten. Colour printing is available via multiple jet configurations using three colours. Printing speeds up to 600 m/minutes have been obtained. Dot resolutions of up to about 240 dots/inch have been achieved with commercially available equipment; this is about equivalent to good-quality typewriting. The process is capable of futher technological improvement and software for half-tone work has recently been announced. About 20,000 ink jet printers have been installed throughout the world and it is likely that ink jet printing will become a major printing process.

Laser electrophotographic printing
A laser electrophotographic printer works from information supplied in digitized form, either online from a computer or offline from magnetic tape. A laser controlled by the digitized data is used to create an image, in the form of a dot matrix, on a photoreceptor belt or drum. The image is then toned, transferred to paper and fused in the usual way. Commercially available machines operate at typically 10,000 − 20,000 lines/minute, producing print of a quality equivalent to good typewriting. A varied array of type styles and sizes can be used. It is possible for each printed sheet to be different from the preceding one. Further developments will enable line drawings and illustrations to be produced. Possible applications include short-run publications, especially those, such as abstract journals, held in machine-readable form for other purposes; another possibility is on-demand publication.

Electrostatic matrix printing
In this process, which also works from digitized data supplied online or offline, the image is formed electrostatically as a dot matrix by a line of print styli. Special dielectric paper is required. Printing speeds of up to 18,000 lines/minute are possible.

Printing specialist fonts
Digitally controlled printers can be programmed to print

specialist fonts, such as Arabic and Kanji. The fonts are software-generated.

Colour xerography

Colour xerography is already commercially available and a laser-driven colour copier has been developed. However there is at present a trade-off between quality and cost or speed. Technically it is possible to produce high-quality colour xerography or electrophotography, but the cost at present is higher than colour photography. The likelihood of high-quality colour xerography or electrophotography being cheaper than colour half-tone printing for longer runs is small during the next decade.

Automation of equipment

Minicomputers and microprocessors are being increasingly used in or with a wide range of equipment, freeing the skilled operator from routine tasks, aiding more consistent results and increasing productivity. Particular examples include electronic composition, the automation of cameras, enlargers and photographic processors, the automation of the setting up and running of the printing press and the automation of bindery operations. Automation of press and bindery operations will have a further beneficial result in that job specification and progress data can be stored and used to preprogram the individual machines, thus improving work organization.

The future of the printed word

During the past twenty years the printing industry has been going through a major change in which time-honoured mechanical processes have been giving way to computer-assisted and electronic methods. The noisy clank of machinery familiar to generations of printers is being replaced by the faint click of electronic machines and the quiet whirr or magnetic-disc drives. Screen-based systems are becoming commonplace. Text and pictures are beginning to be handled in digitized form and integrated with each other. Laser scanning and imaging techniques are being introduced. Digitally controlled non-impact printing process have arrived. In short, the printing industry is adapting to changing technology.

In order to compete with electronic media, printed products will become more colourful, newspapers being a particular example. Lithographic printing processes being increasingly used for newspapers and other work are well suited to producing good-quality colour printing at reasonable cost. The trend toward paperback books and away from hard-cased books will continue. Paperbacks can be economically produced on integrated production lines in which paper, ink and so on go in at one end and printed and bound books emerge at the other; the printing will be done from flexible photopolymer plates. There will still be a market for high-quality books, and these will be produced on machines programmed by minicomputers, controlled by microprocessers and coordinated by computers, to enable the printer to optimize production parameters in his plant and keep costs under control. Short-run text-only publications will tend to be produced 'on demand' by means of digitally-controlled laser printing devices.

The printed word will survive in the foreseeable future. In particular the book will remain — familiar, convenient, lendable and, above all, readable. To borrow the jargon from a rival technology, the book has a future because it is 'user-friendly'.

Acknowledgement

The author wishes to acknowledge the PIRA/PPITB report "Developments in printing technology: a ten-year forecast" as the source of much of the information used in this article.

10. MICROFORM PUBLICATION

S. JOHN TEAGUE
Librarian, City University,
London, UK

Microform publication is but one of the available modern systems of recording and retrieving information conveniently and economically. By definition the words *microform publication* clearly mean publication in reduced format and therefore needing to be read on viewing equipment that will magnify the text back to original size or larger. The term *microfilm publishing* was used in the past by those who wished to stress that the technique was photographically based, but in view of the fact that *microfilm* conjures up the idea of roll film, the term *microform* is to be preferred as all-embracing. Whilst 35-millimetre microfilm will continue to be the microformat for filmed newspapers, periodicals and other large originals such as maps, plans and drawings, so much material is now published on microfiche that this can be seen to be a vital growth medium in publishing.

A microfiche is a small sheet of processed film, positive or negative, measuring 105 mm. by 148 mm. on which reduced images of text appear in a logically arranged sequence of pages. It bears a heading legible by the unaided eye of normal sight. Having an enormous business systems market internationally, microfiche viewing equipment is readily and cheaply available to libraries at about £170 per viewer. Being of simple construction and mass-produced, it has a key place in a highly competitive market and its price is thus about a quarter of that of the roll-film viewer. There has been an immense improvement in recent years in microfiche viewers, optically, mechanically and ergonomically. This has ensured a much more ready acceptance of micropublishing on microfiche than has ever been accorded to the use of micropublications on roll film, for there are many problems involved in reading the latter. These relate to convenience in handling: one nearly always puts the film into the viewer upside down or back to front; one often has to rewind the film before use because neither the last user nor a library assistant has done so: the film is difficult to scan and one often finds that the part one requires to read is at the other end of an unindexed film: if the viewing equipment is mechanized, in many cases one suffers feelings of nausea in viewing rapid film transit across the screen. So, altogether, microfilm in reel form has never been a challenge to the printed word, but rather a necessity, for reasons of space economy, for providing access to heavy bound volumes of decaying nineteenth-century newspapers and other large originals where handling is difficult, and for providing ready acquisition of otherwise unobtainable back runs of periodicals, just to quote a few examples.

Micropublishing, then, will continue to develop on 98-frame microfiche produced, according to the appropriate standards, such as British Standard 4187, "Specification for Microfiche", on archivally permanent silver halide safety-film stock. Where compilations, sets or series are micropublished the introductory material and the index will continue to be published in printed paper format, for there is no point in restricting access and the vast treasures to be published in this way must be accessible by browsing. To which vast treasures do I refer? Well, we are just now reaching the time when the dreams of some of the early proponents of microform publication are possible of fruition. The dream was of a whole library housed in a catalogue cabinet. Now the multiplication of access to whole libraries of material by the relatively cheap process of replication on microfiche followed by widespread sale and dissemination is possible. A library, it must be remembered, has not only the intellectual value of the sum of the printed books that it contains, but also the product of the factors of selection and collection building that make it what it is. Undoubtedly there is a growing market for micropublications of specialist library collections which cannot be served by reprinting, for the costs could not be met. There are, of course, problems relating to copyright, and these, and the problems arising for publishers and authors from the ease with which copying from microforms can be done, would take more space than can be spared here. I have discussed these and related matters in my publication *Microform Librarianship* (Teague, 1979).

There is a pressing need for conservation of the treasures of the printed word that are safely housed in our national and other great libraries but which are printed on paper now fast decaying. There is, now, more than one possible method of conserving these by re-recording them in another medium. The problem with the computer and silicon-chip-based methods is that high technology is involved and the world will increasingly need cheap simple solutions to problems such as this one: solutions that do not require power sources more sophisticated than a simple light source and do not require expensive technical staffing to facilitate output. Micropublishing is one low-technology solution.

As to new publications, the printed word will, in my view, continue to be the major medium of information transfer and it will be paper-based for the foreseeable future. There are many reasons why this should be so, not least the reason that the author wishes, even subconsciously, for the widest possible circulation for his work. The need for the intervention of technology between reader and book at the time of reading reduces the readership. I believe that printing is still the cheapest method of publishing for large volume circulation. At least one advertiser of a word processor has used the 'superfluous carbon paper' approach to promotion. This is not valid, for it will depend upon circumstances, location and size of the operation, as well as purpose. Thus there are many circumstances where printed-paper publications will always be appropriate in the future, as now, and circumstances where the printed word will best be published in microform.

In recent years we have witnessed two developments in periodical and learned-journal publishing using microfiche. These are *synoptic publishing* and *simultaneous publishing*. Synoptic journal publishing is the term used to indicate that kind of journal, now a growing number, that publishes, in print-on-paper format, only synopses or extended abstracts of scientific, technical or other articles. An adequate means of reference is provided by which the reader can request the full article; this he does only if he needs it. The text is prepared from camera-ready copy produced on an electric typewriter. This has the great merit of removing the backlog of papers that journal editors commonly accumulate, awaiting publication (there will still be some delays due to necessary refereeing procedures); it is cheaper to produce than a standard journal, being less bulky, and it is author-prepared. The back-up is normally a microfiche copy of the full article requested, photographed directly from the author's typescript. At first there is usually some resistance on the part of authors who naturally wish to see their hard-conceived technical articles actually in print. However, abstracting and indexing services cannot omit suitable articles just because of their publication format, so *academically* it counts as full publication. The future will show multiplication of synoptic journals as print costs rise.

Simultaneous publication refers to the method of photographing the printed text of a journal immediately after it is published and supplying microfiche copies as required. Obviously the microfiche copy is not actually quite simultaneous in appearing with the printed copy. By use of airmail, however, the microfiche edition can travel, as an air letter, more rapidly across the world than can a printed-paper journal. Thus one advantage of a simultaneous publication system is speed in reaching overseas readers. Another major benefit is that libraries usually purchase the microfiche edition as well as the paper copies, retaining the former indefinitely, thus saving on binding and storage costs.

In the book-publishing world, 'traditional' publishers are not about to be taken over by upstart micropublishers. Wisely, however, one after another they are investigating micropublishing possibilities for additions to their lists, appointing people with knowledge and expertise in this area and taking their first steps into the field. Publishing is publishing, whatever the format, but, certainly, one needs to be well-informed before adopting techniques new to one's own experience. As to sources of guidance, there are two major independent bodies: there is the Microfilm Association of Great Britain, actively informing in this area by conducting an annual micropublishing seminar and publishing a quarterly journal, *Microdoc*; there is, too, the

National Reprographic Centre for documentation, at Hatfield, which, *inter alia*, evaluates microform viewing equipment in a thoroughly objective, useful way.

There are now very many reprints in microfiche format of books long out of print. The economic factors in this area of very low runs are most favourable to the publisher for these are purely bonus sales to libraries, and a publisher's list need never suffer deletions about which there is the slightest doubt as to sales.

There are a growing number of books and periodicals published with a microfiche housed in a pocket affixed to the inside of the back board or cover. This can contain, as in the case of certain journals published by the American Mathematical Society, detailed mathematical or other data to be read in conjunction with an article in that issue by those who so wish. It can be, as in the case of some American book publishers, the full text of the book, to enable libraries either to retain the microfiche and lend the book or vice versa. It can be a compilation of additional material, such as coloured illustrations, supplementing the text of the book in a way that would unduly raise its price above the level of its proposed market if printed as part of the book in the ordinary way. Many conference proceedings now carry, published on microfiche, the full text of papers delivered, or even to be given, with abstracts only in printed-paper format.

The 'microfiche book' is a development that has come to stay, for it is convenient to handle and can be stored among 'normal' books on shelves. Basically it is a booklet made up of microfiche storage envelopes and pages of printed text. If one remembers that each microfiche will carry 98 pages of text, or 209 if it is computer-output microfiche, it can be appreciated that a booklet of very few leaves can represent or be equivalent to a large publication. There will be a printed cover, a title page, a contents page, editorial material and index.

Having mentioned here the two types of microfiche likely to be met with, I feel that it should be pointed out that one needs a microfiche viewer with lens-switching facility from 24-times magnification (that used for ordinary 98-frame microfiche) to 48-times magnification (that used with computer-output microfiche). It is true that some computer-output microfiche is produced at 42-times reduction as this is a function of the computer apparatus used, but in any case it can be read at the 48-times magnification which is now rapidly becoming standard. Ultrafiche, with its higher cost and need for a 'dedicated' viewer of 150-times magnification, need not concern us, since it will not be a developing micropublishing format. There is no great merit in ultra-high reduction, for the additional space saving is negligible whilst legibility can be impaired by specks of dust.

It can be said that the majority of *new* works appearing in microform are published in that way for very special, usually self-evident, reasons. This can only be considered a criticism of micropublication in the one particular that applies to any non-book form of information transfer, that is to say there *is* no other method as acceptable as reading from the printed page. This is not just a subjective comment; it is also the reaction of the marketplace. We do, however, need to utilize the most suitable method in each case. The reasons, then, that are behind decisions to publish in microform now, and that will be there in the future, are closely related to economic factors, ease of access, demand, ease in updating, and type of original material. Any one or all of these reasons can be a most firm indication that microform is the best or only viable way to publish that particular material.

Photographic supplies costs in micropublication are low relative to paper and printing, but it must be borne in mind that the editorial, indexing and promotion costs are similar to those for ordinary publishing. Detailed costings of any system need to be regularly updated, and, in the case of micropublication, for example, it should be remembered both that the cost of film is at present rising rapidly *and* that the film costs do not form a high proportion of micropublishing costs.

Microform publication provides ready access to material that would not otherwise be generally available. It proves to be an excellent means of publication for compilations of multi-format material such as art exhibition catalogues, radio scripts, reports, theses and data compilations. In the realm of data services where continuous updating of information is essential, such as in legal, professional practice and financial compilations, microform publication has become the established competitively priced medium, normally utilizing microfiche. It is common for such data services, where they are published, to specify a particular microform viewer from a particular manufacturer as being desirable in order to produce the best result, whilst being careful to add that other reading equipment will also suit. This is not a restrictive trade practice, but rather standard business enterprise, for a special price, perhaps discounted at up to 25 per cent is usually quoted for the viewer specified. Two examples of this sort of promotion are those for Whitaker's *British Books in Print* and *Barbour Design Library*, both on microfiche.

As an indication of the space saving capacity of micropublication, the *Barbour Design Library* contains, currently, some 58,000 pages of data on some 800 microfiches filed in a unit some 7 in. by 6 in. by 10 in. As an indication of a new technology promoting an existing one, there cannot be a better example than the computer-output microfiche service of *British Books in Print*. Against all the predictions in the trade, booksellers, clearly not among the most opulent people in business, purchased microfiche readers and subscribed. The microfiche service being more rapidly updated than the printed issues could ever be, coupled with it being the first complete listing of British books regularly to reach many of the shops, it must be actively promoting sales of printed books.

The fact that a large organization might have much of its vital data computer-based, with access terminals in ready profusion, does not mean that microform systems will not, or should not, also play a large part in the business concerned. Computer storage of large bodies of information remains relatively expensive; its database remains relatively inaccessible in multi-site operation in that it requires transmission, and, in this connection, Post Office lines are expensive as well as now having a gestation period of six months from order to installation. Microfiche sent cheaply by post and updated replacement microfiche issued only for those parts of the data that has changed is the cheaper option.

Parts lists from industrial organizations such as Lucas and British Leyland used to be printed; the resulting bulky publications were sent at considerable and rapidly increasing cost to agents and dealers all over the world. Now micropublication using microfiche has almost totally succeeded print on paper as the medium used in the electrical and motor industries worldwide. This trend will not be reversed and the future will show a phasing out of those systems that photograph from printed or typed originals and a massive development of computer-output microform in its place. As in the case of 'conventional' micropublishing there are awaiting general adoption international standards that will enable the achievement of the most acceptable output for the reader. In using computer-output microform, publication in this area has bypassed use of the printed word to adopt a technology that does not involve the text ever having been printed or typed on paper. It is keyed in to the computer, checked on a screen, and published on film (usually microfiche), having been directly imprinted on film perhaps by laser beam.

Whatever we may think of this, the workplace of the future will largely deal with its documentation thus, electronically, with the output on screens of one sort or another and the data, both published and internal, on film or other new storage media.

If microform publishing is as advantageous as its promoters argue, if it is as widespread, even ubiquitous, in all areas of information transfer as I have suggested in this chapter, why then is this book published by means of the printed word on paper? Firstly, microform publishing, of its inherent nature, is an obstacle to widespread readership in a mass market. Nobody will voluntarily read it in preference to the same text printed on paper. Secondly, in spite of the enormous growth in micropublishing, many reading environments, such as the home, the bus or train, the small branch library, the small office or other workplace, do not possess microform reading equipment.

I am reminded that, in 1836, when Charles Dickens's novels first began to appear in monthly parts there was, ready waiting, a growing mass readership, hungry for this form of diversion. That is to say a readership for the printed word enthrallingly spun into living narrative. Today the avid mass leisure market is not literate in basis, but graphic, requiring television presentation of dramatic narrative. Television, however, is certainly a graphic medium not suited to reproduction of the printed word and this will impinge upon the future.

If one finds it difficult, unpleasant, or at least unamenable to read from a microform viewer, then one will find it even more difficult, unpleasant and unamenable to read from a television screen or other visual display unit that flickers. Already the trade unions, encouraged by the Health and Safety at Work Act, lay down conditions for the use of VDUs. At least the microform viewer now has a highly controllable static image, although earlier models did not. Thus although, in terms of technique, one could hold that microform publication is an interim technology, it may also be that computer-produced text and other television-type displays of data are also interim technologies.

Combined technologies are likely survivors, with indexes held on computers and electronic searching facility of microfiche-held data coupled with paper-based printout of quite specific information. It is simplistic to see man's communication techniques as in a progression, each new successful device superseding the last. The concept is not valid in any aspect of life. In a real world one hopes that techniques will be used in applications in which they excel, complementing, not entirely superseding, existing systems. So microform publishing, as well as conventional print on paper, will continue. It is rather more likely that the present elephantine centralized computerized data systems will end, and more locally controllable mini- and micro-computer systems will survive. Certainly the existing and future wealth of the printed knowledge and wisdom of the world will be microfilmed and stored and accessed in all sorts of ways, some not yet conceived. Above all, the printed word will remain, for there is no reason why we should ever cease to benefit by use of a major faculty that is so pleasantly personal to each reader and yet so generally available to mankind at large.

References

Microdoc, the Journal of the Microfilm Association of Great Britain, 8 High Street, Guildford, Surrey GU2 5AJ, England. Vol. 1, 1962 to date, quarterly.

Teague, S.J., *Microform Librarianship*, 2nd edition, London: Butterworths, 1979, pp. 67-77.

11. A NOTE ON VIDEODISCS

YURI GATES
PIRA, Leatherhead, UK.

What is a videodisc? The simple answer is that it is rather like a gramophone record with ultrafine grooves; it can be played on a special turntable connected to a television set to give pictures and sound. The real answer is much more complex. Well over forty videodisc systems have been developed or proposed. Not all of the discs are of the conventional circular shape — rectangular 'discs' are also being developed.

How are videodiscs made? This obviously depends on the particular system being used, and it is beyond the scope of this note to describe them all. In the MCA process, the material for the disc is first recorded on videotape. The photosensitive surface of a glass disc is then exposed with a laser beam which is modulated by the signals recorded on the videotape. The disc is then etched so that it has a series of depressions or 'pits' corresponding in analog form to the video-signals; these 'pits' are arranged in a spiral track and are short near the centre and longer near the outer edge. There are 'land' areas between the pits. From the glass disc, multiple copies of the etched surface are made by a nickel-plating process. The nickel replicas become the surfaces used to stamp individual videodisc sides for mass production. After the addition of a reflective coating, the two sides of the disc are joined together to form a single two-sided disc.

During playback, a laser beam 'reads' the information encoded on the disc — light is reflected from the 'land' areas but not from the pits. The optical signals thus obtained are an analog of the original video-signals and can be reproduced as a picture on a television screen.

During playback in the Philips/MCA system, tracking proceeds from the innermost to the outermost track. The disc rotates at constant speed, so the linear tracking speed increases as the tracking head proceeds from the innermost to the outermost track. One revolution of the disc corresponds to the production of one frame on the television screen. The disc has about 50,000 tracks, corresponding to 50,000 frames, and plays for 30 minutes per side. The Magnavision videodisc player being test-marketed in the US enables each individual frame to be located by simply keying a number. The frame can be 'frozen', that is, held stationary. There is also the facility for either forward or reverse slow-motion playback. Since there is no mechanical contact between the tracking head and the disc, there is no danger of the disc surface wearing, even if the 'freeze-frame' facility is repeatedly used.

Philips have produced digitally encoded, as distinct from analog, discs. The digital coding is more compact, which means that for a given size of disc, a longer playing time is possible (up to 60 minutes per side). The player must have a constant linear speed instead of a constant rotational speed, which means that the 'freeze-frame' facility must be forfeited.

Other manufacturers use different methods of producing videodiscs. They also utilize different playback principles. The Thomson-CSF readout system employs optical transmission, rather than optical reflection, which has the advantage that the disc does not need to be turned over to play the second side.

One of the problems for the user of videodiscs is that the systems developed by the various manufacturers are not compatible; discs from one manufacturer cannot be used on players from another manufacturer. However the major competitors are moving toward standardized systems, as shown by the recent announcements of agreements between Philips/MCA and Sony on patent sharing and between Matsushita and JVC on readout systems.

There is one further and significant factor relating to videodiscs which must be considered. Not only can the discs be used for playing back pictures and sound on television sets, but they can also be used for random-access, mass storage of information. If digital encoding is employed, the videodisc can be used instead of a magnetic tape or magnetic disc in a computing system. The accuracy with which data can be recorded on a videodisc is not in itself likely to be high enough for data processing purposes, but Philips have recently developed a Direct Read After Write (DRAW) process which enables data to be verified immediately after recording. Any incorrect data are identified and rewritten on another part of the disc. Data cannot be erased, but access to them can be blocked by deleting the address from the computer's memory. The capacity of the disc used in the Philips DRAW system is currently about 10^{10} bits per side. Research is under way to extend the capacity to 10^{11} bits per side and this is by no means the upper limit of the technology.

What does the development of videodisc technology imply for the printed word? The answer must be twofold, depending on whether videodiscs are considered as devices for playing back visual television-type material or as mass storage devices. As playback devices, they will compete directly with certain kinds of books. Although it is expensive to produce a videodisc master, the actual discs themselves are very cheap, so videodisc publishing is geared to long-run mass production. Videodiscs give motion pictures and sound, as well as colour. However the detailed quality of the picture is not so good as with colour printing and the standard of presentation of text is very crude in comparison with print. One can, however, envisage that they could compete successfully with books in particular areas, for example with children's books, where storytelling in sound with moving pictures would have appeal; books for do-it-yourself, cookery, gardening and hobby enthusiasts where motion pictures could be used to demonstrate practical points; and educational and travel books, in fact generally where moving colour illustrations could be particularly important or appealing features, or the addition of sound could be an asset. Costs of videodiscs are likely to be comparable with or lower than those of books provided sufficiently long runs can be made.

Videodiscs with the freeze-frame device may also compete with certain types of textbooks and reference works. One could envisage a disc containing a teaching programme with moving pictures, or encyclopedia-type material from which individual pieces of information could be selected and displayed on the television screen by the use of the freeze-frame device. The possibility of giving slow-motion demonstrations of particular features to be observed or points to be learned might appeal to those concerned with education and training.

Videodiscs as mass storage devices are unlikely to compete directly with books. Although it has been predicted that the 18 million volumes of the Library of Congress could be stored on 100 optical videodiscs by the mid-1980s the mind boggles at the eye-screwing effort of reading all this on a television-type screen or terminal of current design. Videodiscs in this role are in competition with microforms rather than with the printed word.

To sum up, videodisc technology has advanced to the stage where practicable systems are being put on the market. Videodiscs will probably be sold at prices at or below those of equivalent types of books and they will compete with certain types of books, especially where colour and illustrations are important. It may soon become possible to put whole libraries on videodiscs of the mass storage type, but it seems more likely that this type of application will be mainly archival, and will not compete with primary publishing of books and other printed matter.

References

A. Horder: Videodiscs — their application to information storage and retrieval. NRCd, Hatfield, Herts., 1979.

C.M. Goldstein: Videodisc technology and information systems. Paper presented at the Third International Online Conference, London, 1979.

M.Y. Gates: Video cassettes and videodiscs. In: *Printing technology forecast: a 10-year forecast for the printing and publishing industry*. PIRA-PPITB, Leatherhead, Surrey, 1979.

12. THE FUTURE OF THE PRINTED WORD: ECONOMIC AND SOCIAL FACTORS

A. J. MEADOWS
Professor, Department of Astronomy
and History of Science,
University of Leicester, UK.

Introduction

The way in which technological innovation affects, and is affected by, the economic and social environment in which it occurs is an important question, but also, unfortunately, a complex one. It is important because the likelihood of an innovation being accepted or rejected depends to a significant extent on the environment in which it appears. It is complex because an innovation can itself change the ambient socioeconomic climate and so lead to powerful feedback effects.

The printed word has been around for a long time and so represents an influential factor in the environment encountered by current innovations in communication. To analyse the resultant interaction in detail would require much more than a brief essay, so I shall begin in a roundabout way by sketching a few parallels between innovation in communication − in the sense of transport − and in the communication of information. My purpose is simply to illustrate the range of effects that need to be examined in looking toward the future.

Transport and transport networks have expanded continuously over the past couple of centuries. However, underlying this relatively smooth growth in the total volume there have been major fluctuations in the fortunes of individual categories of transport. For example, extrapolations for the volume of traffic on London streets, made at the end of the nineteenth century, predicted reasonably well the actual flow half a century later. Yet immediately related extrapolations − concerning, say, the amount of horse dung that would need to be removed from the streets — failed badly, because the predominant mode of transportation had changed. This is one aspect of a more general point: innovations are usually seen, at least in their initial stages, as extensions of existing technology. For example, early railway carriages looked much like stagecoaches, because the railway was seen as providing a service like that provided by stagecoaches. It took some little time before carriages that were geared specifically to the requirements of transport by rail appeared. Stagecoaches and trains were in direct competition. The advent of the railway inevitably led to the disappearance of the stagecoach. Such direct conflict does not necessarily occur between all modes of transport. Thus trains and buses can co-exist because they cater, at least in part, for different publics. Finally, new modes of transportation, when they first appear, are often subject to limitations of a technical or financial nature. The people operating the new system are expected to adapt their work habits to the requirements of the machinery. Later, especially if labour costs rise relative to equipment costs, the machinery is modified for the greater convenience of the operatives. A good example is the way in which train-drivers' accommodation has improved since railway engines were first introduced.

Parallels to these transport examples can readily be found in the world of communication. Thus we can talk of the continuous growth over the past century in the amount of scientific and technical data in circulation. Yet there has been a significant changeover during the latter part of this period from handling and storing via the printed word to computer-based handling and storage. We can then point to the use of the television screen for purposes for which it was not intended. Though well adapted for the presentation of pictures, it is, for example, less well suited to the provision of alphanumeric material, but it is currently being used for just such a purpose, because this new need has yet to be fully comprehended. Thinking next of competition between communication channels we can turn to computer networks. These are becoming a major alternative to the printed word in providing bibliographical access to the research literature. At the same time, computer networks are not yet in competition with the printed word as a provider of the research literature itself. Finally, when computers were first employed in data processing, the cost of the hardware and its maintenance was such that computer personnel had to adapt their activities to the requirements — and especially the programming requirements — of the machine. The costs of hardware and maintenance are now falling so rapidly in comparison with those of software and personnel that computers are being increasingly built round the needs of their users.

In technical terms these various parallels illustrate the point that a technology assessment exercise can be carried out under much the same headings regardless of the technology under discussion. In considering the future of the printed word, we can employ a simple assessment technique that works quite well for both communication and transport. This takes into account three factors: trends, channels and items transferred — remembering that our particular interest in the latter two cases is in change.

Time-scale

We can begin by asking what time-scale of change is likely to interest us. It is easy enough to obtain a rough estimate of the number of books, journals, and so on which have been appearing over the past few decades. When plotted as a cumulative number against time, these typically show some kind of exponential, or hyperbolic increase. The interesting time-scale for change with such a curve is likely to be the equivalent of a doubling period. Depending on the particular type of printed communication under consideration, this typically lies in the range 10-20 years.

If we consider changes in other aspects of the print production process, we might well get quite different results. For example, the number of lines of type that could be set per minute increased quite slowly over the period 1850-1950. In the thirty years since then, it has shot up, with an average doubling time of much less than a year. If we wish to look at this aspect of print-on-paper production, ten years is obviously a long time.

But typesetting is a change occurring within the organization of the present printing industry: the general reading public do not notice it as a major innovation. If we restrict our attention to technological changes that directly affect the public – for example, by offering an alternative to the printed word – we can gloss over variations in rates of change. The initial impact of such a 'public' innovation depends on the period required for full-scale marketing plus general acceptance. This is rarely less than a decade. As an example, we can take television which, in some senses, offers an alternative to the printed word. In the US, where acceptance was most rapid, it took a period of somewhat over ten years for the percentage of households with television sets to increase from ten to ninety.

We can now argue in reverse. If it requires a decade for a major innovation to be completed, then a ten-year time-scale for forecasting has one great advantage. Any innovation which is likely to make an impact during that period is already in existence at the time of the forecast. In looking at the effects of new technology, it therefore makes sense to limit predictions of the future of the printed word to the 1980s.

Trends

The first step in this discussion is the examination of current trends. The most evident result is that, on most quantitative assessments, the printed word is undergoing a boom. The world book production figures have been rising at an average rate of 3-4 per cent per annum over the past two decades. It is true that there have been marked differences between countries, and variations in the annual rate in any individual country. (US production has tended to race ahead, whereas the USSR and Japan have tended to slow down.) However the overall growth rate has remained reasonably steady, despite these fluctuations. Similarly, journal titles worldwide have consistently expanded in number during the past twenty years. It is true that not all printed material has shown this rapid growth, for in developed countries at least, newspaper circulations have risen only slowly (or have even decreased). In general terms, however, production of the printed word is quite definitely still expanding.

At the same time, costs are escalating. Labour-intensive activities in the printing and publishing industries have shown particularly steep increases. In consequence, book and journal prices have been going up at a faster rate than many consumers can stomach. Nor have these price increases been accompanied by any increase in efficiency from the viewpoint of the general public. International distribution of books and journals, for example, is not obviously better now than it was twenty years ago.

We may compare these trends for the printed word with corresponding trends for the electronic transfer of information. The latter has been expanding much more rapidly in recent years — albeit from a smaller initial base. For example, the growth of data traffic via computer terminals in Europe approached 20 per cent per annum during the latter part of the seventies (and this was still less than the rate of increase in the US). There have been two main reasons for such quick growth. One is the rapidly increasing utility and convenience of computerized data handling. The other is the rapidly decreasing cost, both per use and in terms of capital and running costs for a given capacity. This latter point can be illustrated most effectively by comparing the capabilities of the ENIAC computer of 1945 with a Hewlett Packard hand calculator of 1975 (Table 1).

Table 1. Comparison of the ENIAC computer (1945) with the Hewlett Packard hand calculator (1975).

	ENIAC	HP-65
Word size	10 decimal digits	10 decimal digits
Data memory capacity	20 registers	9 registers
Program memory capacity	750 instructions	100 instructions
Cost	$480,000	$795
Power required	50,000 watts	0.5 watt
Size	4,000 cubic feet	26 cubic inches

Apart from the cost factor, such equipment also acts to speed up the transfer of information. The advantage in terms of rapid dissemination offered by radio waves over the printed word is too obvious to need comment. But direct competition with the printed word has become more immediate with the advent of high-speed fax. This can transmit the exact appearance of an article or book with much greater speed than any physical transfer.

Alternatives to the printed word

Our discussion of trends indicates the reasons why alternatives to the traditional book or journal are currently a matter of intense concern. Production costs of print-on-paper have been growing rapidly, whilst neither handling nor speed of dissemination has improved in the last couple of decades. In comparison, the electronic transfer of information has become much less expensive, handling of data has improved markedly, and speed of transmission is high. One can readily envisage some kind of crossover point where the virtues of the electronic system outweigh those of a printed-paper system.

Inevitably, the situation is less simple than this suggests. As we have noted, the efficiency and cost-effectiveness of print-on-paper processes have increased considerably in recent years. In particular, much effort is going into the use of computers for the handling of material that will eventually appear in a traditional format. The question to be asked is therefore not the global query — Will electronic media replace the printed word? — but rather, in any given context — What is the likely future balance of advantages between new media, traditional print-on-paper, and some mix of the two? Hence an assessment of new technology and its impact needs to be done case by case, or, at least, category by category.

For the purposes of a brief analysis, we can use a simplified categorization by content. We will divide all information into three categories — entertainment, reference and educational.

In terms of the growth of electronic media, we could say that the expansion of television viewing in the past couple of decades corresponds to a growth in information transfer predominantly relating to entertainment. More recently, a new entertainment aspect of television has appeared: the use of the television screen for playing games. This is worthy of separate mention because it introduces a new communication element — an interactive capability.

Another new form of interaction is teletext, which satisfies the need for selected entertainment information (football results, horoscopes and so on) as well as for instant news. The next step beyond this in entertainment is to link the television screen (or some other VDU) to a personal computer. This could be used, for example, to select and store particularly satisfactory recipes — effectively creating a personalized cookery book — as well as for highly complex games.

Teletext seems likely to provide an acceptable add-on capability. It is simple to use and the customer is only required to pay a single purchase fee. The latter is also true of personal computers, though here the increased complexity of the interactions required may well act to limit the number of interested purchasers. In Europe, at any rate, the signs are that teletext offers no problems, in principle, to the average television user; but personal computers — even if their prices fall as expected — will remain suspect for some time to come.

For some social groups, the past growth of television use may have been at the expense of time devoted to reading the printed word. Thus the financial problems of newspapers and some weekly magazines have occasionally been attributed to the provision of news and discussion programmes on television. Yet, in some areas, television and the printed word have clearly supplemented each other, rather than competed. Bestsellers lists now always contain titles which tie in with television programmes. There is no reason to suppose that an expanded market in videocassettes or videodiscs will change this situation in the near future. Reading continuous text from a television screen is distinctly unsatisfactory, so novels, for example, will continue to be most easily read in traditional book form. Hence, so far as information relating to entertainment is concerned, electronic media are certain to expand their capabilities. This may simply provide new opportunities for the printed word, rather than replace it in any major way.

The effect of new technology on reference information may be noticeably different. Consider, for example, the transfer of secondary services from the printed abstract journal to the online computer file. The rapid expansion in the amount of published research over recent decades has made the handling and retrieval of information from printed sources increasingly time-consuming. In consequence, computer handling and storage has become increasingly attractive. The demand for a transition from one to the other is by no means unequivocal. Whether, or not computer handling is currently regarded as preferable may depend, for example, on the way in which computer charges and overheads are allocated by the accounting system of an organization. Computer retrieval may be only marginally worthwhile in a university environment, say, whilst fully viable in industry. The result is that secondary services are in a transition period, when both print-on-paper and computer access have to be provided. The problem is that dual production may make both channels financially vulnerable during this transition.

Viewdata systems at home, or in the office, face the same sort of viability problem. The question is whether potential customers will prefer to retrieve information via their television screen or via the printed page over the next few years. The answer will depend on the customers' willingness to interact with a computerized system of this type, and on the range of data that it can make available. The starting-up period, which we are now in, is obviously of crucial importance. Can the system take off sufficiently quickly to prevent withdrawal of support by data suppliers? It is already apparent in the UK that some reconsideration of the viewdata audience may be needed because, for example, supply of information to the office may be a better financial starter than supply to the home.

Word-processing equipment, as applied at present, is mainly an ancillary to the production of print-on-paper; but, like most information-handling devices, it can be used for more than one purpose. More particularly, it can be employed as a device for the rapid retrieval of information, either from in-house files or from a central computer. This additional usage is at present parasitic, in the sense that the word-processing equipment is purchased for, say, typing standardized letters, and is then additionally employed as a retrieval device. In the UK, for example, law firms are acquiring word processors for the production of legal documents. It has consequently become a viable proposition to provide legal databases for processing on the same equipment, a development which may have significant implications for legal publishing.

The last of our three categories was educational. To some extent this overlaps with reference, but at least two aspects deserve separate attention — textbooks and specialized research publications.

A multimedia package could quite conceivably replace the textbook — one possibility would be the development of the videodisc for this purpose. As with reading for entertainment, however, it is dubious whether lengthy stretches of continuous prose will appear as anything but print-on-paper in the near future. An historical circumstance — the publishing industry's unhappy experiences with programmed learning in the 1960s — may also dampen enthusiasm for experimentation in this area. More immediately, the considerable capital tied up in textbooks will tend to slow down any change. So textbooks may provide an excellent example of a print-on-paper product that is likely to resist rapid modification.

Specialized research publications are another matter. Although changes in production methods (for example camera-ready copy) have made it possible for research journals to survive with lower circulations than hitherto, small research communities are experiencing increasing difficulty in publishing their work. One suggested solution is that electronic journals should be established for the transmission of short texts. For longer texts, one possibility is the establishment of a system of on-demand publishing. It is, however, still an open question whether either of these developments would be socially or financially viable.

Suggestions for on-demand publishing typically revolve round the use of microform. Although microform can hardly count as a recent innovation, its position as a medium for communication is still evolving. Its progress reflects an interesting change of opinion — which may also hold for other, more recent innovations in communications. When microform first appeared it was thought to be in direct competition with print-on-paper; now it is more often seen as a valuable supplement for use when print-on-paper would not be viable.

The future

The foregoing section has suggested briefly some contexts for encounters between the printed word and various alternative media. We now consider possible implications of these encounters.

The most obvious is that a move toward electronic media is simultaneously a move toward interactive use. Information retrieval via a home television set could simply be the first step along this road. A data terminal in the home could also, in principle, be used for message transmission — replacing the present mail service — or for financial transactions. This range of possibilities has led to a current debate on the future use of the home as a communications and information centre. The creation of such 'centres' is clearly a long-term aim, but even gradual movement toward such a goal has considerable implications for the printed word. As with television, the problem is not so much destruction of print-on-paper communication: rather there is a growing need to be clear what the printed word provides that other media cannot. Correspondingly, the growth of new technology will increasingly demand a multimedia approach to communication, with special problems being likely to arise at interfaces between the media. The printed word will, in any case, be handled for most operations in computerized form — hence it will necessarily be involved in multimedia operations. This will allow both decentralized monitoring of the material via computer terminals and automation of operations currently requiring human intervention (such as checking of spelling).

The long-term implications for the labour force in the printing and publishing industries are therefore considerable, even if the printed word continues at a high level of production. One obvious likelihood is the occurrence of redundancies as a result of increased efficiency. The recent disputes at UK national daily newspapers over the introduction of new technology reflect the fears this is currently raising amongst the work force; but the deskilling of printing and publishing tasks will be as important as redundancy for people working in the industry, both employees and employers. For the latter, a particular problem must be the extent to which the growth of a multimedia approach will lead to diversification of the publishing enterprise, and so how, and when, new types of firms will overlap traditional publishers in their range of interests.

A move toward electronic media will affect not only printers and publishers, but also consumers of the printed word — more especially, libraries. The nature of this impact will depend on the type of library, but, in all cases, usage of new technology should help to reduce pressure on space — currently a major problem for librarians. The most important long-term question will concern the usage of libraries. If information-seeking activities are increasingly transferred to the home or office, will the demand on library services fall significantly?

The rate at which new technology is introduced during the rest of this century will depend as much on economic and social factors as on the appearance of additional technological innovations. This is obviously true of innovations in general, but the exact factors involved vary from field to field. For communications technology, the problematic areas lie especially in the legal domain.

There is first the general question of copyright. This poses difficult enough problems for the printed word, where the matter has been under discussion for centuries. How the concept of copyright should be applied to the operations of new technology is still an open question. Pressures, particularly arising from photocopying, have been sufficient to cause a number of countries to reconsider their position on copyright recently. Differences may well arise between countries, and these will act to slow down international communication via the new channels. The same effect may be produced by disagreements between the PTTs themselves, and between PTTs and other bodies over their exact relationships. Since most

PTTs are in some sense agents of the state, expansion of the new communications technology may also raise the question of state involvement in information transfer much more acutely than before.

The current volume and complexity of communications traffic indicates the central position of information in modern society. Until two centuries ago, all societies were predominantly agricultural. With the advent of the Industrial Revolution, the labour force came to be employed mainly in manufacturing. Now, in most developed countries, communication in its various guises is becoming one of the largest consumers of manpower. One result is that the pressure is now on to use communications personnel more efficiently. The computerized dissemination of information has been one necessary consequence. As with the earlier transition to an industrialized society, the development of a computerized society is likely to be encouraged by its growing financial viability, but, correspondingly, may lead to significant social problems.

Summary

It is quite obvious that the electronic transfer of information will continue to expand rapidly in the 1980s. The new strand for this decade will be the diversification of channels through which the information is disseminated. This expansion does not imply an immediate decline in the output, or diversity, of the printed word (though in terms of the communication system as a whole, print will become somewhat less important). One reason is that much of the new technology, for example word processors and intelligent copiers, simply enhances the efficiency of production of the printed word. Hence, during the 1980s, we can expect the significant changes to be in the way in which the printed word is produced and transmitted, rather than in the amount of print-on-paper in circulation. For the immediate future, therefore, new technology implies the redistribution of manpower at least as much as a decline in demand for manpower. Since redistribution leads to a requirement for different skills, however, this could mean redundancies in some parts of the work force and shortages in others.

Electronic information transfer has been a minority interest to date, both because of the expense of the equipment involved and the complexity of handling it. The most important advance of the 1980s may be the familiarization of a much wider range of people with the process. One reason is the continuing decrease in cost of the equipment. During the 1980s, most of the equipment needed for basic information handling should fall into the same price bracket as a television set. At the same time, there will be a clear trend toward 'user-friendliness' − the provision of software that can be used by people with little knowledge of computers.

Much of the interest attached to information in the home falls in the 'entertainment' area, as we have seen. Despite the potential size of this market, the important information consumers of the 1980s may rather be in the business community. The growth of office automation that will undoubtedly occur during the coming decade, although intended initially as a method of enhancing in-house efficiency, could well lead to a more generalized concern with information transfer. If so, the 1980s may see the business world pioneering an interactive multimedia approach to communication.

The overall result at the end of the decade should be an enhanced awareness among the general public of available information transfer techniques. A question of considerable interest will be the response of the printing and publishing industries to this awareness. Will these industries, based on the printed word, diversify to become multimedia enterprises, or will the new needs be satisfied by the growth of a new industry?

13. SCIENTIFIC AND TECHNICAL PUBLISHING IN THE 1980s

A. K. KENT
Director, Information Services,
The Chemical Society, UK.

Introduction

All the evidence suggests that prophecy is an unrewarding activity, but few can resist the temptation to peer more or less knowledgeably into the future even when they recognize the dangers. The success rate for prophets is low. Nevertheless, having accepted this invitation to speculate on the appearance of scientific and technical publishing in the 1980s, I suppose I must attempt to do so.

There are a number of possible approaches to crystal-ball gazing. The technologist is inclined to produce a menu of all the marvels that are in store for us — a sort of 'chips with everything' approach. The sociologist will give great weight to human and environmental factors and, since his political leanings will tend to be to the left, will discount such trivial considerations as money and resources. The egotist will tell you what he wishes to see happen, with scant regard to the evidence, and with a firm conviction that the mere act of prophecy, by him, is sufficient to bring the projected events about. There will be elements of all three of these approaches in what I have to say, though, if pressed, I would have to concede that the major thrust of my observations can probably be categorized as socio-egotistical.

The possibilities afforded by technology

There can be no doubt that the 1980s will offer a fine harvest

163

of technological marvels. Microprocessors will become more and more powerful, cheaper and cheaper (in terms of capability per pound sterling) and smaller and smaller (the mini-, micro- and nano-chip). It will, undoubtedly, be possible to offer computing power comparable to that of some of the largest present-day computing installations in the space occupied by a domestic television receiver and at about the same price. There will be parallel developments in the evolution of storage devices, both for digital and analog information. We can expect to see the giga-byte store with random-access in microseconds following the trend of the last decade. Particularly, I believe we shall observe great advances in capability, usefulness and economy of analog storage devices like the videodisc and the development of technology for providing rapid access to information stored in this form.

Terminals will increase in sophistication and capability so that the rather primitive 'dot-matrix' terminal will be replaced by terminals with full graphics capability at prices comparable to, or lower than, those of today's 96-character displays. I believe we may see both voice-producing and voice-responding terminals becoming available at prices within the range of ordinary mortals.

Telecommunications capabilities will increase both in availability and in traffic-handling and may be cheaper. It is at least conceivable that the combination of all these good things will finally bring us to the reality of a computer on everyone's desk and in everyone's home (this latter, no doubt, tastefully styled to match the early Victorian decor that seems likely to be our fate at that time).

In terms of hardware then, we shall have capabilities undreamed of twenty years ago and difficult to visualize even today. These capabilities could be applied in a host of mind-boggling ways to the task of acquiring, storing, retrieving and disseminating information. The technologists would have us believe they will be thus applied, and, moreover, that by doing so we will be capable of achieving, or at least approaching, the nirvana of instant access to information at trivial cost. However, the naivety of technologists and their inability to perceive the real nature of the world in which their wonders will perform is well-known; we would do well therefore to pause and consider those nasty, unpredictable, human and environmental factors that will blunt the cutting edge of technology and disturb the elegance of their solutions to our problems.

The human and environmental factors

There must be few scientists and even fewer technologists who do not, from time to time, regret that people do not behave like machines. But, as they say, 'There's nowt so queer as folk'. Though technology has an inevitable tendency to spawn further technology there have been few cases where the direction of technological advance (or perhaps I should say change) has been successfully forecast, except in hindsight, because of the queerness of folk. In examining the perturbations that will disturb the advance of information technology it is useful to divide people into two broad classes, the creators and the users, and consider some of their needs. Amongst creators of information we should perhaps distinguish between those whose creation enters the public domain and those whose light remains hidden beneath a bushel. I shall say nothing of these latter since they have little relevance to a discussion of scientific and technical publishing. The creators of public information have as their main interest its widest possible dissemination. From this dissemination they expect to enjoy some kind of reward. The form of the reward is, superficially, varied and complex but (and perhaps I could be accused of undue cynicism in saying this) almost always resolves itself into a monetary one. The university- or industry-based research worker publishes in the hope that his status (and hence value) will be increased in the eyes of his peers. The publisher of a patent hopes to establish an 'unfair' advantage over others who might wish to exploit a particular invention. The greatest benefit will come, potentially, from the widest possible dissemination. Any system of publishing which reduces the perceived width of dissemination will be resisted. However irrational he may know his reaction to be, will an author in fact find it as ego-enhancing to put his work into a computer store from which it may or may not emerge as the result of the machinations of information scientists as he does to see it 'in print' and to know that it is in print in 500, 1,000 or 5,000 replications.

The situation is more complex for users of information. There are, to begin with, more classes of users than of creators. The needs of the intermediary and the ultimate user, the scholar and the industrial researcher, the bench scientist and the research manager may be, and I think are, very different. A solution which satisfies the needs of one will not necessarily satisfy the needs of the others. It seems to me that there is a growing divergence between the needs of these various classes of users and hence a requirement for a greater variety of ways to retrieve, disseminate and present information. In industry, for example, the demand is for rapid access to directly pertinent information at the lowest possible cost. In the academic world there is much less stress on the need for currency and a different, broader view of what is pertinent. The industrial user often complains about the mass of poor-quality or irrelevant information that has to be screened out and asks for mechanisms which will reduce this; the academic user seldom expresses this particular concern. The information intermediary looks for structure in his sources of information and an organization of it that will ease the difficulties of finding what is wanted even if using such a structure and organization requires a level of skill only possible for an expert. The rest of us want to get at information without needing a deep understanding of the techniques of indexing or search strategy formulation or whatever.

Bridging these two groups are the information processors, the publishers, database producers, information brokers and their like. This information industry provides the mechanisms which serve the needs of both the creators and users of information and does so in order to make profit (whether the organization concerned is in the profit or the not-for-profit sector). In earlier days there was an essentially simple and straightforward relationship between the creators of information and the users of it through the intermediation of a publisher concerned with the interests of both parties. In the last ninety years and especially in the last decade we have seen the growth of a wide spectrum of 'parasites' upon this simple relationship who have, with the best possible motives, sought to improve the service available to users of information. In so doing they have distanced the creator of information from the user and, though they have undoubtedly added value, have added to costs. Though this development may have been an inevitable consequence of the growth of information it has had the unfortunate effect of breaking up the process of transmission of information from creators to users into a plethora of competing systems with often conflicting interests.

The future of the printed word

I must, finally, come to the point. What can we expect the world of scientific and technical publishing to look like in the 1980s?

Broadly, I believe, it will be not much different from today except in one regard which I shall come to in a moment. The predominant mechanism for transfer of scientific and technical information will continue to be print on paper. The creators of primary information will resist, and successfully, any attempt to replace the convenience and the ego-enhancing qualities of the printed page in the conventional scientific journal by any presently foreseeable substitute. There will be a continued but slow evolution toward newer styles of primary publication like the synopsis journal but only so long as these retain a significant element of print on paper. Microform will not develop as a significant alternative to conventional methods of publishing though it will have some importance as a mechanism for reducing storage costs for archival material. The electronic journal will not be realized in its fully computerised form. There will, however, be components of the electronic journal concept that will be adopted by publishers in an effort to reduce costs and increase revenue. These will include the capture of primary information in machine-readable form so that editing and preparation for publication can be speeded up and photocomposition techniques can be used. Publishers will seize on the opportunities afforded by the possession of a machine-readable record of the primary literature to reprocess and repackage the same information in a variety of guises to increase revenue. As a result the duplication of information will increase, with the same information appearing in a number of different places at different times.

In the field of secondary information we shall see a significant move away from the printed abstracting and indexing publication toward the online-accessible database. But this will not lead to a reduction in costs of access to secondary information for a number of reasons. The activities of the publishers of primary information will increase the difficulties of identifying duplicate information and add to cost whether the duplication is eliminated or allowed to pass through unidentified. Primary publishers will be increasingly concerned to protect their property rights and prevent secondary information sources from exploiting primary information. We have already seen indications of this phenomenon in the field of business information and it will surely spread into other areas of technical and scientific publication before long. But perhaps most significantly the secondary information producers will be increasing the royalty charges made for use of their databases as an offset to loss of revenue from printed versions of their services. I expect that we shall see charges made for use of the major databases increase by between three and ten times in real terms over the next decade. These increases will more than eliminate any cost savings arising from lower computer or telecommunications costs.

The one way in which the 1980s will differ from the 1970s in a major way is that there will be a very much less orderly system for information transfer. The potential for exploitation in a variety of ways that comes from capturing information in machine-readable form will be recognized by a very much larger range of people. Many new things will be tried, often without adequate planning or thought for their impact on the information transfer system as a whole. When this phenomenon is coupled to the increasing awareness, of both creators and manipulators of information, that information is a commodity from which it is possible to make money we have the seeds of instability. I fear that this instability will become manifest in the first half of the next decade, with a rapid increase in the cost of use of information and the collapse of some and possibly many of the established institutions and practices in the field without the compensating replacement of them by effective alternatives. While the end result may be a new and more cost-effective information technology I doubt that we shall observe this renaissance in the next ten years.

I should conclude, I suppose, by offering some thoughts on how these gloomy predictions might be prevented from becoming reality. I must say frankly that I do not see what can be done to prevent it. To be brutally frank I believe that the control of the mechanisms for information transfer are moving ever more rapidly out of the hands of the responsible into the hands of the irresponsible. This transition is being fuelled by increasingly unrealistic demands for information at ever lower cost and by the accelerating application of inappropriate technology. Long-term stability and orderliness is being sacrificed to short-term gain. This is hardly surprising in a general political and social environment which sees no harm in seizing the immediate advantage and letting the devil take the future. Perhaps the only possibility for ensuring that my scenario turns out to suffer the fate of all prophecy is for the major creators, processors and users of information to get together to understand each other's problems and develop together a common strategy for development and advance. We are in the same boat together. If technology and the opportunity it offers for the future causes us to run before we can walk then none of us may pass the finishing line.

LEARN WITH BOOK

R. J. HEATHORN

A new aid to rapid — almost magical — learning has made its appearance. Indications are that if it catches on all the electronic gadgets will be so much junk.

The new device is known as Built-in Orderly Organized Knowledge. The makers generally call it by its initials, BOOK.

Many advantages are claimed over the old-style learning and teaching aids on which most people are brought up nowadays. It has no wires, no electric circuit to break down. No connection is needed to an electricity power point. It is made entirely without mechanical parts to go wrong or need replacement.

Anyone can use BOOK, even children, and it fits comfortably into the hands. It can be conveniently used sitting in an armchair by the fire.

How does this revolutionary, unbelievably easy invention work? Basically BOOK consists only of a large number of paper sheets. These may run to hundreds where BOOK covers a lengthy programme of information. Each sheet bears a number in sequence so that the sheets cannot be used in the wrong order.

To make it even easier for the user to keep the sheets in the proper order they are held firmly in place by a special locking device called a 'binding'.

Each sheet of paper presents the user with an information sequence in the form of symbols, which he absorbs optically for automatic registration on the brain. When one sheet has been assimilated a flick of the finger turns it over and further information is found on the other side.

By using both sides of each sheet in this way a great economy is effected, thus reducing both the size and cost of BOOK. No buttons need to be pressed to move from one sheet to another, to open or close BOOK, or to start it working.

BOOK may be taken up at any time and used by merely opening it. Instantly it is ready for use. Nothing has to be connected up or switched on. The user may turn at will to any sheet, going backward or forwards as he pleases. A sheet is provided near the beginning as a location finder for any required information sequence.

A small accessory, available at trifling extra cost, is the BOOKmark. This enables the user to pick up his programme where he left off on the previous learning session. BOOKmark is versatile and may be used in any BOOK.

The initial cost varies with the size and subject matter. Already a vast range of BOOKs is available, covering every conceivable subject and adjusted to different levels of aptitude. One BOOK, small enough to be held in the hands, may contain an entire learning schedule.

Once purchased, BOOK requires no further upkeep cost; no batteries or wires are needed, since the motive power, thanks to an ingenious device patented by the makers, is supplied by the brain of the user.

BOOKs may be stored on handy shelves and for ease of reference the programme schedule is normally indicated on the back of the binding.

Altogether the Built-in Orderly Organized Knowledge seems to have great advantages with no drawbacks. We predict a big future for it.